"Ch

Peter Sander,

the

IT'S *just* LUNCH!®

guide to
dating
in Atlanta

the

IT'S *just* LUNCH!®

guide to
dating
in Atlanta

by **Michelle Brown** &
the dating experts at It's Just Lunch

FROM THE EXPERTS AT IT'S JUST LUNCH
RESPONSIBLE FOR OVER **2,000,000** FUN FIRST DATES

10 Finger Press
Wellington, FL

The It's Just Lunch Dating Series
includes guides to dating
in these locations:

America
Albany and Saratoga
Albuquerque
Atlanta
Austin
Baltimore
Birmingham and
Huntsville
Central Pennsylvania
Charlotte
Chicago
Cincinnati
Cleveland
Dallas
Denver
East Bay
Honolulu
Houston
Kansas City
Las Vegas
Los Angeles
Milwaukee
Naples, Ft. Myers
and Sarasota
New York City

Northern New Jersey
Northern Virginia
Orange County
Orlando
Philadelphia
Phoenix
Pittsburgh
Raleigh-Durham
Sacramento
San Antonio
San Diego County
San Francisco
Seattle
Silicon Valley
Singapore
South Florida
Southeastern Michigan
St. Louis
Tampa
Toronto
Twin Cities
Washington, D.C.
Western New York
Wilmington

Acknowledgements

Special thanks to Michele Gough and Mahesh Grossman
of The Authors Team for their help in
organizing this book.

The It's Just Lunch Story

When founder Andrea McGinty's engagement was suddenly called off, she began the tedious search for a way to meet "normal," well-educated professionals. The ideal date, she decided, was a lunch date. In 1991, McGinty launched the company's first office in Chicago. The premise was simple: a dating service based on a personalized screening and a painless meeting with her to determine whether she had the type of people the client would like to meet.

It's Just Lunch caught on quickly! The company has over 70 offices worldwide, with new locations added nearly every month. These offices cater to an upscale audience of over 30,000 clients. Most clients have college degrees and many have a graduate degree.

The total results are astonishing: over two million fun first dates and thousands of marriages.

Their secret to success? Founder McGinty's certainty that when you explore enough avenues to meet people, "there's absolutely somebody for everyone."

www.itsjustlunch.com

Contents

dating for busy professionals®

Chapter 1

Change Your Outlook and Your Luck Will Change

Here you are, about to start your great dating adventure. You've been dreaming about meeting someone special for a while now, but the idea of actually getting out there and doing it is a little scary.

You spend time and energy on your career, your workouts and your finances, and now you're ready for romance. You've tried the traditional ways to meet new people — blind dates set up by friends, the Internet, the bar scene. But none of that has worked out. The next step is to go out into the world and meet new people, but where and how? You're busy and don't have a lot of time for trial and error.

That's where we come in.

There is no better place to find good advice about dating than from people who have gone through it before — in our case, more than 50,000 times a month. *It's Just Lunch* is responsible for millions of fun first dates, so we know a thing or two about successful dating.

How to Use This Book

In each chapter, we'll demystify some aspect of the dating process, as well as provide tips and suggestions to boost your prospects. At the end of each chapter, we'll point you in the right direction with a current list of the best places to date or find dates in Atlanta.

Welcome to the Wonderful World of Dating

Perhaps you've picked up this book because you recently went through a divorce or a breakup, or maybe you've been single for some time and just haven't met the right person yet. Whatever brings you here, let us first say, congratulations on being single. Yes, we mean it! Being single is an exciting time in your life. It's a chance to learn more about yourself, to understand what you want for the future, and to discover the qualities you'd really like in a partner. And you're in for a treat — there are a whopping 110 million singles in the United States to choose from.

Of course, not everybody has a positive outlook on singledom. In fact, some people are downright negative, especially about dating. If you think like this, you might want to take a look at how you could be sabotaging your chances. Are you the type who loses hope if a date turns out not to be what you expected? Do you judge every date as a marriage prospect? Do you try so hard to impress that you end up scaring the other person away? If this sounds like you, chances are you take dating way too seriously.

It's hardly unusual. These days we're inundated with reality shows and movies that depict two incredibly beautiful people meeting for the first time, barely getting to know each other, quickly falling in love and then deciding to spend the rest of their lives together. With expectations like that, it's no surprise that we're all wondering, "Where's mine?"

In addition, chances are you've been hurt or suffered some pain or loss along the way. The idea of facing that ordeal again is enough to make you want to stay in bed with a good book and a pint of Ben and Jerry's Chubby Hubby ice cream.

If you're reading this book, you probably *do* want to date. If you're not feeling enthusiastic yet, you might need a little attitude adjustment to get you mentally prepared for your dating journey. Having a positive outlook as well as knowing the pitfalls and how to overcome them will make all the difference.

Start by putting all those bad relationships and dates from hell behind you. That's all in the past, and you can't do anything about them. Think about the *future* and make a promise to give yourself the time to enjoy the dating process — and try not to take it too seriously.

Here's the scoop: Dating can and should be lots of fun. Keep this in mind and you'll have a much better time than you think.

Successful Dating Guidelines

The key to successful dating is to focus on enjoyment and friendship. Date with the intention of making a new friend rather than expecting to meet your life partner. You'll have more fun and way less "performance" anxiety.

Six Ways to Maximize Your Fun

1. Approach dating as not just looking for an important relationship, but as enjoying life.
2. View dating as a chance to increase your circle of friends.
3. Find innovative and unusual places to meet people. Join a club, volunteer or take up a sport.
4. Take one positive aspect away from each date. For example, "I liked his values, her sense of style or his humor." Pick a quality or characteristic that you would like in your future mate. This benefits you, even if you aren't attracted to that person.
5. Become the person you'd like to date. Use your experiences as an opportunity for personal growth.
6. Embrace your singledom. You have the freedom to do anything you want, meet everyone you want and learn everything you can about yourself.

The point is to keep dating light and casual, especially early on. On a first date, go out to lunch, drinks or brunch and split the check. This keeps the expectations and pressure lower. If you decide to see each other again, you know your date is interested in you.

It's that simple.

As you get to know each new person, you'll have an opportunity to "try each other out" and see if the relationship might work. Pay attention to what you're discovering. As you progress on your dating journey, you'll be exposed to new types of people and new ideas. Even if a date doesn't develop into a full-blown relationship, you're still growing and learning as a human being, which makes life interesting and exciting.

If dating still sounds daunting to you, keep reading. You'll find many suggestions throughout this book that will make it easier than you imagine.

Breaking "The Rules"

The first and only rule we have here at *It's Just Lunch* is to throw out all your old ideas and rules about dating!

Dating is not about playing games, using clever tactics or making sure you come out on top. There are no winners and losers as far as we're concerned.

While other guides might instruct you to hold out, be mysterious and develop a game plan to trap your mate, we don't believe in that. Those games don't work in the long run and they're exhausting. If you present a fake exterior and try to be someone you're not, you deny yourself the opportunity to be liked for who you really are. And that's what real love is all about, folks — just be yourself from beginning to end!

DON'T:

- Play games
- Play hard to get
- Pretend you're not interested
- Wait three days to return his or her call

In other words, don't utilize any other ploy that seems like game playing.

Dating Karma

It's true — what you put out is what you get back! Whether you believe in the whole principle of karma or not, the idea behind it makes sense. If you are constantly thinking you're too fat, too skinny, too old, too poor, too stupid or too anything to attract a love match, chances are you probably won't.

If you believe there are only jerks, gold diggers or messed up freaks out there, these are the people you will meet. If you think dating is a complete waste of time, then it sure as heck will be! Negative thoughts produce negative results. It becomes a self-fulfilling prophecy.

If this sounds like you, then make a promise to yourself to stop it RIGHT NOW! When you catch yourself in a negative thought, give yourself a little pep talk. Say, "stop," and turn the thought around to something more positive such as, "I'm hot, smart and one helluva catch." You get the idea.

Would *You* Date You?

Think about it. Would you? This is a very important point. Unless you become the type of person who you're looking for, you won't attract the type of person you seek.

Have you ever known men or women who aren't necessarily the most handsome or pretty individuals, but they never lack dates? What makes them so attractive? You guessed it: self-confidence, and it's contagious. It also screams sex appeal. These folks are glowing with a bright, friendly, fun attitude, and they have a genuine interest in others. They're happy with who they are and appreciate what they have to offer. This positive energy attracts an abundance of people who want to meet them.

Self-confidence produces the most amazing results. Here's why:

- It's sexy!
- It allows you to relax and have fun.
- It means you take rejection lightly and not personally.
- It makes it clear that you are not desperate.
- It means you're content with yourself, your looks and your life — which only makes you more attractive.

In order to gain self-confidence, you must first learn how to love yourself. It's important that you recognize and appreciate what's great about you — and accept what's not so great. If you don't love and accept who you are, how do you expect someone else to?

DO the Following for Yourself

Try these six boosters to improve your self-confidence and sex appeal.

- Stop measuring yourself against others, especially celebrities or fashion models. Recognize that you are a hot ticket with a unique set of qualities and attributes. If you believe you are special, you will attract a partner who appreciates what you have to offer. Tell yourself, "I'm great just the way I am" or "I'm exciting" or "I'm loveable." You are! This kind of pep talk helps imprint positive messages into your brain and eventually will change your outlook.

  Remember, the very characteristic or behavior that turns one person off may turn another person on. Don't waste your time with people who don't recognize what you have to offer. Learn to love yourself for everything you are and everything you're not. When you like who you are, people will naturally be drawn to you.

- Surround yourself with people who treat you with the love and respect that you deserve. If you have people in your life who are overly critical or negative, weed them out.

- If you're not happy with the way you look, treat

yourself to a new look. Join a gym and get in shape. You'll feel like a million bucks. Dress and act your best at all times, because you never know when you might run into your dream date. When you look good, you feel good too.

- Step outside your own boundaries. Join Toastmasters, take a dance class or a stand-up comedy class, go horseback riding or parachuting. Push through your fears, and you'll find yourself alive with confidence.

- Finally, date more. As you handle all the different situations you come across, it will reinforce positive feelings about yourself and boost your confidence in your dating ability.

At the end of the day, everybody could use a little improvement. But nobody's perfect and no one ever will be, so you have to balance your desire to be all that you can be with your willingness to accept who you are.

Know What You Want: If You Build Them, They Will Come!

When you're looking for that special someone, you need to figure out who this person is going to be. Knowing what you want and who you're looking for really helps you find the right person.

We once attended a seminar on relationships where attendees were asked to design their perfect mates as specifically as possible. The goal was to create a wish list of all the qualities and characteristics we felt were important. It was a great exercise — a lot of the attendees realized that they didn't know what they wanted, although they had very specific ideas of what they *didn't* want. A few months later, the participants reunited to complete the final part of the seminar, which analyzed our results. We were blown away by how many participants had met people who matched most of the criteria on their list. It was as if putting it down on paper reinforced the belief in their mind's eye. Or perhaps by defining what they wanted, they became more conscious of those qualities when they saw them in a potential partner. Either way, this exercise worked for a large number of people.

Visualizing your ideal partner and the relationship you want is a great motivator. Athletes have long understood this process of imagery and will visualize a goal before acting on it. You can do the same with your love life. Give it a shot now! You have nothing to lose.

Close your eyes and picture your ideal partner. Engage all your senses. How does this person smell? What does he or she look like? Listen to this person's voice. How does it sound? When you kiss, how do you feel? Where are you? What are you doing? Are your friends and family around? How does he or she interact with them? Try this a few times until the picture becomes clear, then take out a piece of paper and make a list of the most important characteristics of this partner.

List about 20 qualities that mean something to you. What values and attributes does this person have?

Look over your list and separate your "deal breakers" from your "ideals." "Deal breakers" are the absolute non-negotiable traits, like finding a partner who wants children or is of the same religion (if those traits are important to you). "Ideals" are more about the attributes or traits you'd prefer, like "ambitious" or "good sense of humor."

By prioritizing which qualities are important and which are ideal, you'll discover what you're absolutely unwilling to accept and where you've got some flexibility.

Be Flexible

Don't be overly specific when you think about your ideal partner — such as wanting "tall blonds" or "no bald guys."

Celebrate individuality and be open to new possibilities. You could end up ruling out the woman or man of your dreams simply because they have the wrong hair color or are a few hairs short. Remember, it's a wish list, and nobody's perfect. Over the coming months, it will change and grow as you discover what's really important to you in a relationship. Remain flexible and open with your "ideals."

Fools Rush In

One of the biggest dating mistakes we see at *It's Just Lunch* is when people are in too much of a rush to settle down. Disaster! They hook up with the first compatible person who comes along, instead of dating several people and then making a powerful choice as to what's best for them.

Give yourself time to choose. The dating experience teaches you a great deal about what's really important to you in a partner and what you have to offer. By observing yourself, you will gain new insight into how you react to different situations, and which problems you bring into each relationship. It's only when you are inside the dynamic of a relationship that you can truly discover these things — otherwise it's all "in your head."

Now Get Out There!

Over the years we've met with hundreds of thousands of active daters and heard the inside scoop on just about every dating scenario one could possibly imagine. All of this has provided us at *It's Just Lunch* with the most up-to-date, insightful information on successful approaches to dating, which we're happy to share in this book. But the truth is that all the knowledge in the world won't make the slightest difference in your life, unless you physically get out there and date.

Since you've picked up this book, you're heading in the right direction and taking a proactive approach to meeting new men or women. Now you need to get off the couch, turn off another episode of *The Bachelor* or *Bachelorette*, and get out there and star in your own reality show. Consider these points:

1. Dating is a numbers game. The more potential mates you meet, the more likely it is that you will find "the one." If you're hoping that fate will drop him or her off at your door, think again, unless you have a penchant for UPS drivers.

2. Joining a dating agency like *It's Just Lunch* is not an act of desperation. It's the smartest way to meet the type of people you're interested in. It means you are the driver in your own life, not a bystander who leaves things up to chance.

3. You can get over your ex. Let's face it. If you're still hankering after your last love, then your heart isn't going to be open to meeting someone new. You are emotionally unavailable. Write a note to yourself that reads "single and unavailable" and stick it on your computer. Laugh at yourself. It helps. You'll get there eventually, just give it time. In the meantime, enjoy being single.

4. Dating doesn't have to take a great deal of time. If you're an *It's Just Lunch* member, we set up your dates so you only need an hour for lunch or for drinks after work.

Okay, no more excuses. You can sit back and wait forever or get out there and have some fun!

The Lists

Five Best Places to Boost Your Ego

Studio Oliver Salon
789 Argonne Ave. N.E., Atlanta
(404) 607-9757 • www.studiooliver.com

In the heart of midtown, *Studio Oliver* is one of the best salon/spas in Atlanta—with great hair and skin care lines like *Bumble & Bumble*, *Kerastase*, and *Mario Badescu*.

Bikram Hot Yoga
2000 Cheshire Bridge Rd. N.E., Atlanta,
(404) 636-7535

You're guaranteed a sweaty workout in the 105-degrees required for Bikram yoga. Heat helps prevent injury, so stick your leg behind your head. Don't worry, it won't hurt later.

Spa Sydell
Brookwood Plaza, 1745 Peachtree Rd., Ste. M, Atlanta
Call for other locations.
(404) 255-7727 • www.spasydell.com

Voted the best spa for 2003 by *Atlanta* magazine, *Spa Sydell* offers a full menu of services and a highly trained staff. It's the ultimate in relaxation and pampering.

Concourse Athletic Club
8 Concourse Pkwy. N.E., Atlanta
(770) 698-2000 • www.concourseclub.com

This luxury club offers personal-touch hospitality combined with cutting-edge fitness and sports programming. There's also a full service salon with spa and day care services.

Luna
3167 Peachtree Rd. N.E., Atlanta
(404) 233-5344

Shop 'til you drop. Everything you love—from *Seven, Free People, Theory* and *Michael Stars. Luna* stocks fabulous shoes, the final touch to your dating outfit.

Five Best Places to Sweeten You Up

Dante's Down the Hatch
3380 Peachtree Rd., Atlanta
(404) 266-1600 • www.dantesdownthehatch.com

Wander down the plank into an authentic wharf scene—complete with a full-scale sailing ship—and enjoy Atlanta's best chocolate fondue and cheesecake.

Alon's
1394 N. Highland Ave. N.E., Atlanta
(404) 872-6000

Alon's is a favorite neighborhood bakery serving the best double chocolate chunk cookies, French pastries, and Heath-bar crusted brownies in the city. Yummm.

Paolo's Gelato Italiano
1025 Virginia Ave. N.E., Atlanta
(404) 607-0055

Nothing beats an icy cool gelato on a hot day. Plus *Paolo's* serves its own cannolis.

Bacchanalia
1198 Howell Mill Rd. N.W., Atlanta
(404) 365-0410 • www.starprovisions.com/bacc/menu.html

Crave something exotic? Try the warm Valrhona chocolate cake with vanilla-bean ice cream—it's out of this world.

Joli Kobe Bakery
5600 Roswell Rd. N.E., Atlanta
(404) 843-3257

A Japanese bakery serving *pain au chocolat*? It may sound unusual, but this place creates some of the most exquisitely delicious French pastries in all of Atlanta.

Chapter 2

Where to Begin

With your new positive outlook on dating, a rough idea of what you'd like in a partner, and confidence beaming all over your face, you're ready to take matters into your own hands and venture out to find Mr. or Ms. Right.

So where do you start looking?

Here's what we tell all of our clients: *Try everything out and see which option works best for you.* Each method has its pros and cons, and we'll take a look at those a little later in this chapter. But for the most part, it's vital to just get out there and start exploring your options.

With that in mind, here are four ways you can improve your dating odds no matter where you go:

1. Be proactive

   Most people know exactly what they want out of their careers and have a clearly defined set of goals. But when it comes to finding a partner, it's often left to chance. You'd never be that random with your job! If you really want to find that special someone, make dating as important as your career.

   The first step is to tell everyone you know that you're available. Tell your friends, your co-workers, your hairdresser and the neighbors. Heck, tell the cable guy. Get the word out. Don't make a big deal of it, just casually let them know you're on the lookout for eligible dates, so if they happen to know someone who you might hit it off with... you get the idea!

   If you keep it a secret, chances are you'll be home alone most weekends, so don't be shy, and drop the occasional hint. How else is the world supposed to know?

2. Be open

   The best advice we can give you (aside from joining *It's Just Lunch*, of course) is to be open to meeting someone everywhere you go. There are lots of opportunities throughout your regular day to meet your future partner. You just need to have your radar turned on. Think about it. You could meet her over your morning latte; on the train heading to work; while standing in line for a chicken salad, cruising through the produce aisle, at the dry cleaners or the gym.

Interesting people are all around us, but we're all so consumed with our busy lives that we rarely take the time to look up. So start today! Notice your surroundings and the people who cohabit them. Here's what will make the biggest difference and allow serendipity to do its thing: being aware, keeping a friendly smile on your face and not being afraid to say hello once in a while.

3. Widen your scope
Don't limit your options by thinking someone is not right for you, is beneath or above you, or isn't your usual type. That high-powered corporate attorney who helped negotiate your company's last acquisition might be longing to go out with someone who is creative and free spirited — you!

Don't get turned off because of occupation, income, height, number of children, fitness level, hair color, hobbies, musical tastes, shyness, boldness or whatever. Right now you're just looking for dates — and like job opportunities or taxis — when one appears, a whole slew of others seem to follow. Try not to focus on the ultimate goal, but think more about putting your dating skills into practice and having some fun.

4. Create a ripple effect
Do you know why it's smart to talk to anyone, anywhere, even if that person doesn't seem to be your type? Well, if you throw a pebble into the dating pool, it can have a significant ripple effect that is sure to benefit you.

A 30-year-old female friend of ours recently met a 60-year-old woman at an art exhibition. Even though the older woman was twice her age, the two found they had many things in common, especially their taste in art. The woman later introduced our friend to her nephew and they've been out several times since.

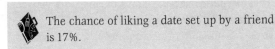
The chance of liking a date set up by a friend is 17%.

Having a genuine interest in getting to know new people and keeping an open mind while you're networking might end up being more valuable than you think. You just never know who that person might introduce you to in the future. Similarly, if you meet someone you like, but you don't feel a love connection, why not offer to set him or her up with a friend?

Never turn down a party invitation or an opportunity to expand your network of friends and potential dates. Seek like-minded people who can introduce you to colleagues of a similar quality. Expanding your network will ensure a life rich with opportunity and happy times.

Looking for Love in All the Right Places
Dating is a numbers game, but the odds of finding the right person increase if you look in the *right* places.

You Gotta Have Friends
Your friends are your number-one resource for finding a mate. Use them. However, don't rely solely on them.

Co-Workers
Just like your friends, co-workers are a great resource for finding possible dates. There are downsides, however. If you and your date end up falling out, or one of you breaks the other's heart, your co-worker could find himself or herself in an awkward position. The best solution is to try to keep the friendship, dating and work issues separate.

Expand Your Possibilities
A circle is exactly that — a circle! And often we get stuck inside our own. There's nothing wrong with that — after all, it's great to have people in your life who you know you can depend on. It's great to have a routine. But that circle can shrink.

While getting fixed up by friends and co-workers is a traditional approach to finding your soul mate, stepping outside of your comfort zone and trying some new dating avenues expands your possibilities and increases your confidence ten-fold.

In *The Artists Way*, creativity coach Julia Cameron states that she often sees synchronicity in the lives of her clients. When they develop a strong commitment to bringing their dreams to life, events around them start to fall into alignment with that vision. Little coincidences take place and lead them toward their true path. For example, a writer meets a producer at a party the day after he finishes his screenplay, or a personal trainer finds a studio for lease the day after she decides to go solo and start her own business.

This happens in love too. It has a lot to do with your *intention*. The moment you become open and accessible to meeting new people, miraculously, potential dates begin to materialize all over the place, often when you least expect it. Your circle expands.

This happens regularly to our clients, the moment they take action and join *It's Just Lunch*. One client, Lisa, went on three dates through our service. Each time we sent her to the same restaurant because it was close to her office and she really loved the atmosphere and food.

Although she enjoyed all three dates, there wasn't a strong love connection and she was happy to continue meeting a few more guys. At the end of her third date, after the man left and she was waiting for the valet to bring her car, Lisa started chatting with the restaurant manager, Brad. Each time Lisa had visited the restaurant previously, Brad, who found her attractive, had his eye on her. Because *It's Just Lunch* coordinators call and make lunch reservations, we become very familiar with many restaurant staffers, who usually take special care of our clients. Obviously, Brad knew Lisa was open to dating. When he saw his opportunity to ask her out for lunch, she was extremely flattered and agreed to go.

Of course, you know how this is going to end, right? Lisa and Brad fell in love and recently were married. Lisa says that just getting out there and being open to dating caused Brad to show up in her life. After all, if she hadn't been on an *It's Just Lunch* date, she never would have met her husband.

Every time you get out of the house and meet someone new, it sets off a domino effect that generates new opportunities.

Let's take a look at some non-traditional methods of dating:

Internet Dating

It doesn't matter if you're having a bad hair day, if you live in the boonies, or if there's three feet of snow outside your window — finding a date now is possible in a 24/7, instant-gratification moment through a slew of online dating services and chat rooms.

This approach to finding a date can be thoroughly enjoyable as long as you don't set your expectations too high. Let's face it, you can't really tell what people are like until you meet them in person — no matter how recent they say their photo is.

The Pros and Cons of Cyberdating

The Pros: It's immediate and convenient. It's cheap! You get to know basic information about your dates before you meet them in person. You have access to thousands of people and can narrow your search by criteria.

The Cons: The biggest con is also one of the most appealing parts of online dating. You can be anybody you want to be and so can he or she. Studies mentioned in *The Wall Street Journal* state that, "30% of online dating site visitors are married and countless others misrepresent themselves." Not exactly what you signed up for, huh? You'll find more than your fair share of untruths online, so don't believe everything you read or see.

More cons: Many Internet dating junkies are not interested in real relationships. Navigating through websites and wading through hundreds of profiles can be very time consuming. Also, safety is a big concern. Without a screening process, you haven't the faintest idea who you might be meeting for coffee.

Yes, it's a shot in the dark, so be prepared for some disappointments. On the upside, your odds are about the same as meeting your ideal mate in a bar, and you don't even have to put on a clean shirt. The best part of cyberdating is that you get to practice your flirting skills. You also get first-hand experience with your cyberdate's ability to string together sentences. By putting yourself out there, you gain more courage to try other ways to meet someone.

Here are a few basics to keep you safe and informed when meeting new folks via the Internet.

Dos and Don'ts of Online Dating

1. DO be honest. You're going to have to meet in person one day (or at least you hope to), so tell the truth early rather than having to face an awkward conversation later.

2. DON'T reveal too much about yourself until you become better acquainted.

3. DON'T use your last name or give out your personal information until you've known the person for a while.

4. DO dial *67 before dialing their phone number. It will block your phone number and name from appearing on a recipient's Caller ID unit. You also can use your cell phone so your address can't be tracked.

5. DO get a separate email account that does not give away your real name — some email providers allow you to create multiple addresses or names for free.

6. DO post an up-to-date photo, and ask if their photo is recent. Many aren't.

7. DON'T spend too much time emailing before talking on the phone or meeting in person. Nothing can replace face-to-face chemistry. Better to find out if you have any before you get too involved.

8. DON'T jump too quickly into sexy talk; it may send the wrong message.

9. DO meet in a public place.

10. DO make every word count. Keep your descriptions light hearted, to the point, and add a little teaser.

11. DO expect a flood of emails. Longtime users will jump at the opportunity to meet someone new.

12. DON'T be ambiguous. Be clear about what you want, your goals and desires.

Speed Dating

This is definitely not for the shy types, or those who take a little time to warm up. Speed dating is like horseracing: The bell rings and you're off! The pressure is on to be the best that you can be in six minutes or fewer. Still, if you want the opportunity to meet a dozen singles in one night, you can do just that.

First, you register online for an event in your city. Most

are held at local clubs and restaurants. Once there, you get a nametag and a worksheet. You then chat with about a dozen other singles in less than two hours via a series of six-minute "speed dates." At the end of the six minutes, a bell rings and you move on to your next date.

You keep track of who you'd like to get to know better, and they do the same on their worksheets. At evening's end, you turn in your worksheet, and if there's a match, the organization sends an email to both with the other's contact info so you can arrange your "first" date. After that it's up to you. Phew!

Dating Services

These services run the gamut, with some offering events, singles' nights and seminars while others provide intro-ductions, video dating, computer dating and matchmaking services. Some focus on fixing up singles who are interest-ed in sports. Others cater to specific religious groups. There are even some for millionaires.

When choosing a service, there are a few things to con-sider to ensure you don't get ripped off or unwittingly sign up with a fly-by-night service. Stick with busy, reputable services, and be sure to ask the following questions:

- How many years have they been around?
- What is their success rate?
- How many clients do they have?
- What are the demographics?
- Do both men and women pay?
- Are people available for questions you might have?
- How responsive are they?
- How many dates are you entitled to, and over what period of time?
- Do they tell you the price over the phone or do they make you come in to find out?

We can tell you all about the workings of one very success-ful dating service: *It's Just Lunch.*

Yeah, yeah, so we're a little biased on this one and who can blame us with a success rate of thousands of mar-riages? We've definitely got something to brag about.

Here's why we're so successful: Everyone has to eat. So why not consider a matchmaker who schedules lunch dates for you? Instead of popping out for a sandwich, you can use your time wisely and have a very productive and entertaining lunch.

Joining *It's Just Lunch* is not as expensive as some of the other professional matchmaking services, whose rates can run as high as $5,000 or more.

What makes us unique is that *It's Just Lunch* does all of the work for you — and we even make the lunch reservation! All of the people you meet will be busy professionals who want to meet singles outside of their office, client list or usual circle of friends. Our roster includes doctors, architects, journalists, engineers, lawyers, TV producers, management consultants, writers, teachers, business owners, advertising execs — and that's just for starters. The best part is that they all have the same objective as you: finding someone special in town.

This is how it works. First, you schedule a confidential interview with us. This no-pressure interview enables us to carefully discern what it is you look for in a potential partner. We talk about what has worked for you in the past (and what hasn't) and what your interests are. We'll know by the end of the hour if we have what you are looking for. If so, the fun begins!

After your date has been hand-selected by us, we will give you a call and tell you all about the person we've chosen. We don't give out last names, phone numbers or places of employment. Once the two of you give us your schedules, we choose a convenient restaurant and set up a lunch date. Sometimes it's a weekend brunch, sometimes a drink after work but never, ever dinner. It's a first date that's short and sweet, which you'll enjoy at one of the many fun, hip eateries on our preferred restaurant list.

Taking this light-hearted approach helps reduce nerves and anxiety so you can relax and enjoy the time together. What more could you ask for? (And no, we don't pick up the tab.)

After the date, we encourage you to call in and provide feedback so we can learn more about what you like and dislike. This helps us fine-tune the matching process.

If you do meet that special someone and decide to date exclusively, you can put the service "on hold" for up to a year. If your current beau fails to measure up, then you simply pick up the phone and we reactivate your membership right away.

Singles Events

When most people think of dating, they think of singles events and singles bars. To find some in your city, check the local paper or try an online search. You can find events in all types of venues from museums and theaters to bars and clubs. The best approach is to go as a non-member and check out the event before committing to a year's membership.

Social clubs are hotspots for active singles, and they offer a good opportunity to meet people with similar interests. It's much easier to strike up a conversation when you have something to talk about. You pay a lower-rate membership fee to participate in fun activities like kayaking, dining clubs, hiking and theater visits — to name a few. Check online to see if a group is available in your city.

The Lists

The Five Best Singles Bars

Hand in Hand
752 N Highland Ave. N.E., Atlanta
(404) 872-1001

An authentic Irish pub with a great jukebox! People flock to this Highland watering hole to meet old friends and make new ones. (Don't be surprised if you have to wait in line!)

East Andrews Café & Bar
56 E. Andrews Dr. N.W., Atlanta
(404) 869-1132 • www.andrewsupstairs.com

This Buckhead bar attracts 30-something professionals. *East Andrews'* open-air courtyard is especially popular in the summer months.

The Tavern at Phipps Plaza
3500 Peachtree Rd. N.E., Atlanta
(404) 814-9640 • www.thetavernatphipps.com

Check out this little jewel of a tavern known for its super-friendly napkin-throwing dish-breaking-bartenders (who bear a striking resemblance to Antonio Banderas).

Goldfish
4400 Ashford Dunwoody Rd. N.E., Atlanta
(770) 671-0100 • www.heretoserverestaurants.com

With superb Cosmopolitans and an amazing seafood and sushi menu, you can't go wrong at *Goldfish*. The crowd is trendy, upscale, and professional.

Front Page News
1104 Crescent Ave. N.E., Atlanta
(404) 897-3500 • www.fpnnews.com

A truly relaxed and laid back café in the ultra-trendy midtown area, offering a delicious selection of New Orleans-style cuisine. Try the Cajun egg rolls or a signature martini..

Five Best Clubs

Club Eleven50
1150B Peachtree Rd., Atlanta
(404) 874-0428 • www.eleven50.com

This aesthetically pleasing converted amphitheater in midtown boasts two full bars, a dance floor, a VIP room, an art gallery, and a patio with a reflecting pool.

The Leopard Lounge
84 12th Street, Atlanta
(404) 875-7562 • www.leopardlounge.com

The *Leopard Lounge* is so midtown. The décor features psychedelic animal prints and the dance floor heaves with Atlanta's most successful and attractive 30-somethings.

Loca Luna
836 Juniper St. N.E., Atlanta
(404) 875-4494

An eclectic crowd frequents this sprawling club. Live greenery, patios and fountains will make you feel like you're in Costa Rica—especially after a few shots of tequila!

Compound
1008 Brady Avenue N.W., Atlanta
(404) 872-4621 • www.compoundatl.com

Known for its "net parties" (single networking parties), this vast club is set amidst some of the lushest landscaping in Atlanta.

Tongue & Groove
3055 Peachtree Rd. N.E., Atlanta
(404) 261-2325 • www.tongueandgroove.com

Drop by and rub elbows with the beautiful people at this hip upscale cocktail lounge and club.

Chapter 3

Places to Go,
People to See

Whether you're heading out for a few martinis with friends, volunteering at the local dog shelter or taking a class in feng shui, you increase your chances of meeting Mr. or Ms. Right ten-fold simply by getting out of the house.

So you've gotten as far as the doorstep — now what? In this chapter we'll take a look at some of best venues to scope out potential dates and offer a few suggestions for making the most of them.

Beyond the Bar

If the bar scene just isn't cutting it for you, we offer a whole slew of fun and interesting activities where you could easily run into your soul mate.

Spend time in places you like, doing the types of things you really enjoy. Choose activities that will put you in a position to meet people who are like you or who at least have similar interests.

Coffee Shops/Juice Bars/Bookstores

Bookstores with coffee shops are great locales to make new friends. Try scoping out approachable people in sections of the bookstore that reflect your interests. With all those book titles, you've got thousands of potential conversation starters. If you spot a hottie, check out the book section he or she is browsing, and if you know something about the subject, speak up. If you don't, pick up a book and ask if they know anything about the author you're perusing. Once you've broken the ice, suggest a move over to the coffee area for some frothy conversation.

Classes and Workshops

Signing up for classes at the local junior college or university is really a win-win situation: you're doing something you enjoy, expanding your knowledge and meeting like-minded people.

If you want to improve your odds, why not join a class that usually is frequented by the opposite sex? Guys, try interior design (it can't hurt), personal development or gourmet cooking. Ladies, look into business, management, computer classes and golf.

If no one in the class catches your eye, don't lose hope. Once you start to cultivate new relationships, these folks will introduce you to their friends and family.

Dance classes are a terrific way to meet other singles and are a whole lot of fun. Country and swing dancing are very popular. How about learning to tango, salsa or meringue? You'll pick up some hot moves, get in shape and best of all, dancing comes complete with partners who often rotate among the class.

Sports Leagues

If you're a sports enthusiast, joining a league is one way to meet other athletic and sports-minded people in a non-threatening environment. Socializing after the game provides further opportunities to meet and mingle, but there are some downsides to the league approach. As with any other bunch that meets regularly, some people won't want to "date" within a group or a team because they are afraid of ruining the group's chemistry.

Golf, tennis, softball and polo are among the best sports to find successful eligible professionals.

Health and Sports Clubs

Fitness-conscious singles invest a lot of time working out by playing sports, visiting the gym or taking fitness classes.

Sports clubs (like a hiking club) and leagues are especially popular with men, so ladies, this is a great opportunity to meet athletic guys. Most of the people you meet at these places are fun. They are outdoorsy, adventurous, often well traveled, fit and outgoing people who love to meet others.

Keep in mind that most members want to meet people who are competent and enjoy the sport, so don't join these clubs unless you have a real interest. If you are a beginner, there are groups and classes for every level to help you master the sport.

Golf is extremely popular these days, and the driving range, clubhouse, pro shop and putting green are great places to come across potential dates. Ski or sailing clubs are popular on both coasts and around cities with large lakes. There are several large ski clubs around the United

States. Many are involved in racing and offer their own leagues and activities.

Finally, there's always the local gym. If you spot someone attractive while working out, ask for advice on toning up your glutes or which cardio machine yields the best results. Stay alert and don't close yourself off to everyone by clamping on headphones or immersing yourself in a magazine while riding the stationary bike.

Wine Tastings and Dinners

If you enjoy the finer things in life, a wine tasting or gourmet dinner event is a great networking opportunity. Most attendees are 40 or over. This typically is a white-collar, professional crowd.

Some groups organize trips to vineyards and others hold tastings in local restaurants. If you really are up for an adventure, you can sign up for a wine-tasting trip to Italy, where you're sure to find romance.

Call some local restaurants that are known for their wine lists and see what events they're planning.

You can also log on to www.localwineevents.com, which bills itself as the "largest wine and spirits calendar in the world."

Volunteer/Fundraisers/Political Campaigns

Did you know that there are volunteer groups just for singles? In many large cities, organizations like the Single Volunteers of New York City or the Leukemia Society of America offer opportunities that bring together unattached volunteers. This is a rewarding way for you to connect with new people who share similar values. You get to make a difference in the world while meeting folks who are also giving back to the community. Search online for "volunteer groups for singles" and enter your city to find local organizations.

If you support a certain political party, you can volunteer to help with campaign efforts. Many cities have a Young Democrats or Young Republicans group. Political fundraising balls or parties that raise money for charities are another great way to meet people and network. Once again, you will encounter people who share your views and you'll build a strong camaraderie as you work together on projects.

Bars and Nightlife

Regardless of how you feel about it, the bar and club scene is still a feasible place to meet other singles. We know several people with happy marriages who met in a bar or a club, but we've also heard quite a few horror stories too. Even though the quality of dates cannot be guaranteed here — and it's more likely you'll find a one-night stand than a lasting relationship — you will socialize with members of the opposite sex, and that alone improves your chances of meeting a new love.

Going out and being social opens up opportunities, so go have some fun — you never know when cupid will strike! As long as you keep your expectations in check and don't confuse that warm heady rush you get after a few martinis with true love, you won't be disappointed.

Though the odds of meeting your soul mate in a bar may not be great, there are some things you can do to improve your chances.

Take time to observe people and don't allow yourself to be drawn to the best-looking person in the room. Instead, sit back and watch how that person interacts with others. Are they friendly, polite, do they seem interested or drunk?

Be open and accessible. Smiling and talking to various people sends the signal that you're approachable.

Bars and clubs, above all, are excellent places to test your conversation and flirting skills, to meet different types of people and observe body language first hand. (See more on this in chapter 4, "The Language of Love.")

Your choice of watering hole is vast, depending on the type of company you'd like to keep. Different breeds of the human species gather at different locales, and frequenting one of those venues will increase your chances of meeting that type. We hate to put people into *types* that frequent certain *types* of bars, but it's true!

Let's look at some of the more common establishments.

The Wine/Martini Bar

If you prefer to focus on conversation and cocktails, then the wine or martini bar is your best bet.
- **Who you'll find there:** Suburban hipsters and professionals, usually well groomed and sophisticated.
- **The Scene:** Swanky and cultured.
- **Dress Code:** Smart/Casual.

The Sports Bar

Catch a game and a buzz as armchair quarterbacks and football maniacs scream instructions at an impressive number of TV screens per square foot.

- **Who you'll find there:** Slightly younger crowd, blue-collar or collegiate sports fans.
- **The Scene:** Lively, loud, lots of woo-hooing!
- **Dress Code:** Casual.

The Hotel Lounge

Settle into a comfy couch, catch up on *The Wall Street Journal*, and tap your feet to the beat of the pianist's background jazz tunes.

- **Who you'll find there:** A more refined crowd; business types on expense accounts.
- **The Scene:** Relaxed and very posh. This is where the wealthy come to sip cocktails in comfort.
- **Dress Code:** Dressy.

The Pub

If you can't get to Dublin, you can find a wee bit o' Ireland in an authentic style pub. If it's not Irish, it's English style, so expect fish and chips, shepherd's pie and plenty of good old-fashioned brews on the menu.

- **Who you'll find there:** Ex-pats from the U.K., Australia, South Africa and New Zealand as well as friendly local natives digging the energy and the accents.
- **Vibe:** A hospitable crowd partaking in the "eat, drink and be merry" customs you'd find in any neighborhood pub anywhere in the U.K. crossed with the casual familiarity of the American "local."
- **Dress Code:** Casual.

The Hot Spot

Ultra cool interiors gleam with modern architectural angles, plush velvet couches, plasma TVs and hardwood floors. Writhing sirens dance on elevated boxes as deejays spin a mix of juicy hip-hop and Top 40.

- **Who you'll find there:** The A-list crowd. You may find yourself dancing next to well-connected nightlife connoisseurs and local and visiting NBA stars.
- **The Scene:** Stylish, sophisticated and sexy.
- **Dress Code:** Designer duds.

The Dance Club

Once past the velvet-rope crush of wriggling bodies clam-
oring to be deemed worthy, the dance club offers infec-
tious beats and eye-candy treats for those who want to get
their groove on.

- **Who you'll find there:** A mixed crowd of young professionals and fabulous hipsters.
- **The Scene:** A well-dressed crowd looking to dance,
  flirt and dance some more.
- **Dress Code:** Sexy

The Lists

Five Best Coffee Shops, Book Stores and Juice Bars

Borders Books, Music & Café
3637 Peachtree Rd. N.E., Atlanta
(404) 237-0707 • www.bordersstores.com
Conveniently located in the heart of Buckhead, *Borders* is
the meeting place of choice for students and intellectuals.
It's also a favorite spot for celebrity book signings.

Starbucks
240 Peachtree St. N.W., Atlanta
(404) 589-4522 • www.starbucks.com
Ah, *Starbucks*! No matter where you are in the world you
know what you're getting—great coffee, and plenty of singles hanging out, reading or working on their laptops.

Arden's Garden
1117 Euclid, Atlanta
(404) 827-0424 • www.ardensgarden.com
Arden's is where the health-conscious crowd gets freshly
squeezed juice, fresh fruit smoothies and shots of wheat
grass. The tangerine juice is phenomenal.

Caribou Coffee
3255 Peachtree Rd. N.E., Atlanta
(404) 261-0020 • www.cariboucoffee.com
There's always a line at the drive-through, but once
inside you'll find the Buckhead crowd relaxing with a
mocha while reading the newspaper or discussing business deals.

Café Intermezzo
4505 Ashford Dunwoody Rd. N.E., Atlanta
(770) 396-1344

The aroma of the finest coffee beans, a chillin' atmosphere, and dim lighting, make this café a hot spot for after dinner conversation and dessert. Try the cheesecake!

Five Best Places to Take Classes

Café Tu Tu Tango
220 Pharr Rd. N.E., Atlanta
(404) 841-6222 • www.cafetututango.com

A Buckhead landmark, this hip club allows 20-somethings to learn slick new dance moves or show off those they already have. It also serves some of Atlanta's finest tapas.

Bikram Hot Yoga
5930 Roswell Rd., Atlanta
Other locations: Peachtree Rd.
(404) 255-9642 • www.bikramhotyoga.com

For those who love a challenge, take a 60-minute class in a studio that's heated to 90-plus degrees. Hot yoga is popular with men and women—but ladies, forget the mascara!

Margaret Mitchell House
999 Peachtree St. N.E., Atlanta
(404) 249-7012 • www.gwtw.org

Where would-be authors indulge their passion for writing. Who wouldn't be inspired working in the house where Gone With the Wind was written? Check website for classes.

How to be Married in a Year
Emory University
1440 Clifton Rd. N.E., Atlanta
(404) 727-6123 • www.emory.edu

Take the bull by the horns and learn a bunch of different strategies for meeting potential mates. You're guaranteed to meet lots of other singles here!

High Museum of Art
1280 Peachtree St. N.E., Atlanta
(404) 733-4400 • www.high.org

Fans of the old masters and modernists alike consider this a great place to brush up on art history and meet other art enthusiasts. It also offers a comprehensive lecture series.

Five Best Sports Leagues

Atlanta Lawn Tennis Association (ALTA)
849 Peachtree Dunwoody Rd. N.E., Atlanta
(770) 399-5788 • www.altatennis.org

Do you dream of playing at Wimbledon or are you just plain fed-up with bouncing balls off a backboard? A place for players at every level, with plenty of eligible, sporty singles.

Atlanta Ski Club
6255 Barfield Rd. N.E., Atlanta
(404) 303-1460 • www.atlantaskiclub.org

This association organizes annual trips to the best ski destinations. Can't ski? Don't fret. The club functions as a social group for active singles and welcomes non-skiers, too.

Ruff 'n Sluff Bridge Club
1809 Roswell Rd. N.E., Atlanta
(770) 973-7717 • www.mindspring.com/~ruffnsluff/

Believe it or not, bridge is hip again! If your mom didn't teach you how to play, *Ruff 'n Sluff Bridge Club* gives private lessons and will help place you on a team.

Sierra Club, Inc.
1401 Peachtree St. N.E., Atlanta
(404) 475-1914 • www.sierraclub.org

This national organization is a favorite for singles who like to explore nature. Whether you're an expert camper or a novice day hiker, *Sierra Club* has a trip for you.

Atlanta Club Sport
6040 Dawson Blvd. Ste. K, Norcross
(678) 994-0793 • www.usclubsport.com

Offering volleyball, flag football, and soccer played on co-ed teams—some with names too randy to print here!

Five Best Health Clubs and Gyms

Peachtree Center and Athletic Club
227 Courtland St. N.E., Atlanta
(404) 523-3833 • www.peachtreeac.com

This state-of-the-art gym, located in the heart of downtown, has a spectacular view of the city. (Many of its members work in the Peachtree Center).

Concourse Athletic Club
8 Concourse Pkwy N.E., Atlanta
(770) 698-2000 • www.concourseclub.com

A luxury athletic club known for its personal-touch hospitality and cutting-edge fitness and sports programming. It also offers a full service salon/spa and day care services.

Jeanne's Body Tech
3165 Peachtree Rd. N.E., Atlanta
(404) 261-0227 • www.jeannesbodytech.com

Choose from lots of fun classes at this Buckhead gym. Although smaller than most, *Jeanne's* equipment is state-of-the-art and the personal training is top-notch here.

Urban Body Fitness
742 Ponce De Leon Pl. N.E., Atlanta
(404) 885-1499 • www.urbanbodyfitness.com

Atlanta's best neighborhood gym, this place is for serious gym-aholics who really want to burn some calories and sweat. Exposed brick walls and steel give it an urban look.

Crunch
3340 Peachtree Rd. N.E., Atlanta
(404) 262-2120 • www.crunch.com

If you simply can't get around the "no pain, no gain" rule, then you might as well do it in style. *Crunch* sets the standard for gyms. You won't be disappointed.

Five Best Bars for Wine, Martinis or Tapas

Noche
1000 Virginia Ave. N.E., Atlanta
(404) 815-9155 • www.heretoserverestaurants.com

This eclectic Mexican bistro in the heart of the trendy Highlands, attracts plenty of young singles during Happy Hour, with its quaint patio and inviting bar.

Café Tu Tu Tango
220 Pharr Rd. N.E., Atlanta
(404) 841-6222 • www.cafetututango.com

A Buckhead hotspot brimming with a colorful, Latin atmosphere. *Café Tu Tu Tango* serves fun tropical drinks and some of Atlanta's finest tapas.

Beluga
3115 Piedmont Rd. N.E., Suite B101, Atlanta
(404) 869-1090 • www.beluga-martinibar.com

Where affluent singles stop for a drink between visits to
Bones and the *Ritz-Carlton Buckhead*. A cool martini bar, a
fabulous atmosphere, and live jazz on weekends.

Joel
3290 Northside Pkwy., Atlanta
(404) 233-3500 • www.joelrestaurant.com

This chic, sophisticated restaurant has been featured in
Gourmet and Esquire. It serves some of Atlanta's finest cuisine and is a popular choice for special occasions.

Dailey's
7 International Blvd. N.E., Atlanta
(404) 681-3303 • www.daileysrestaurant.com

Famous for its cigar selection and signature martini menu,
Dailey's has an atmosphere reminiscent of the Sammy,
Dean, and Frank era. Enjoy a martini and the live jazz.

Five Best Sports Bars or Pubs

Taco Mac
1006 N. Highland Ave. N.E., Atlanta
(404) 873-6529 • www.taco-mac.com

An inviting neighborhood patio draws sports fans from all
over the city. Wearing red and black will guarantee you a
beer and a seat among the crowds of Georgia fans.

Frankie's Food, Sports & Spirits
5600 Roswell Rd., N.E., Atlanta
(404) 843-9444 • www.jocks-frankies.com

If you're looking for a slightly upscale sports bar, then
Frankie's is your place. The walls are laden with more signed
jerseys and sports memorabilia than you can take in.

Three Dollar Café
3002 Peachtree Rd. N.W., Atlanta
(404) 266-8667 • www.threedollarcafe.net

Three Dollar Café features a great selection of beer on tap
and great American appetizers. All the action happens on
the patio.

ESPN Zone
3030 Peachtree Rd. N.W., Atlanta
(404) 682-3776 • www.espnzone.com

ESPN Zone is the ultimate sports bar! The state-of-the-art TVs and the fantastic sound system will make you feel like you're actually at the event you're watching.

Champps Americana
7955 North Point Pkwy., Alpharetta
(770) 642-1933 • www.champps.com

This hot spot attracts singles and families alike for great food, spirits, and team camaraderie. Thursday nights feature Karaoke.

Five Best Restaurants

Bacchanalia
1198 Howell Mill Rd., Atlanta
(404) 365-0410 • www.starprovisions.com/bacc

This comfortable, chic restaurant (in midtown's west end) is one of Atlanta's best. Featuring seasonal chef's choice cuisine and a fixed price menu that changes daily.

Goldfish
Perimeter Mall, 4400 Ashford Dunwoody Rd. N.E., Atlanta
(770) 671-0100 • www.twist-restaurant.com

Seafood, steak and sushi are perfect for an after-work meal on the patio, or a date at the full-service sushi bar. Impeccable service in a trendy, fun and aquatic atmosphere.

Joel
3290 Northside Pkwy, Atlanta
(404) 233-3500 • www.joelrestaurant.com

Serving some of Atlanta's finest cuisine, this is a favorite among the trendy and sophisticated. Offering delicious French fusion cuisine and an extensive wine list.

Dish
870 N. Highland, Atlanta
(404) 897-3463

You'll blow your date's mind at this stylishly converted gas station, sporting exposed brick walls with black and white photography. Try the rosemary pine nut popcorn!

Portofino
3199 Paces Ferry Pl. N.W., Atlanta
(404) 231-1136 • www.portofinobistro.com

For a taste of Tuscany right here in Atlanta, enjoy the patio of this converted house and order calamari, a Mediterranean pizza, and a bottle of Chianti. *Appetito buono!*

Five Best After-Hours Spots

Majestic Diner
1031 Ponce De Leon Ave., Atlanta
(404) 875-0276

This local landmark is a great place to enjoy breakfast and hot black coffee in the wee hours of the morning. Try the pork chop and eggs with a pecan waffle!

OK Café
1284 W. Paces Ferry Rd. N.W., Atlanta
(404) 233-2888

Drop by late and join the Buckhead party crowd for a burger or a blue plate special and all the coffee you can handle.

Red Light Café
553 Amsterdam Ave., Atlanta • www.redlightcafe.com

Located in the Midtown Outlets, the *Red Light Café* is great place for a late night latté. A full-service bar is also available.

Club 112
2329 Cheshire Bridge Rd. N.E., Atlanta
(404) 261-0155

If you can get through the legendary line, you can join hip-hop's *in*-crowd and dance the night away at this contemporary urban club.

Electra
3081 E. Shadowlawn Ave. N.E., Atlanta
(404) 627-8464

Stop by this Buckhead retro-lounge for a blueberry mojito, a mint julep, or a champagne cocktail. (Open until 3 A.M. Tuesday through Saturday.)

Five Best Happy Hours

Rock Bottom Restaurant
3242 Peachtree Rd. N.E., Atlanta
(404) 264-0253 • www.rockbottombrewery.com
Equipped with famous in-house brewed beer on tap and pool tables. A great spot for Buckhead professionals to hang out and relax after a long day at the office.

Rio Grande Cantina Restaurant
3227 Roswell Rd. N.E., Atlanta
(404) 237-3227 • www.riogrande.com
Make sure to drop by the large outdoor patio for an icy Margarita! This popular Mexican restaurant is especially fun on Cinco de Mayo.

Neighbor's Pub
752 N Highland Ave. N.E. Ste. C, Atlanta
(404) 872-5440
Trendy and crowded, *Neighbor's Pub* is all about the deck. Come early to guarantee yourself a seat!

Atkins Park Tavern
2840 Atlanta Rd. S.E., Smyrna
(770) 435-1887 • www.atkinspark.com
Atlanta's oldest continuously licensed tavern is a neighborhood pub with plenty of beer on tap, good tunes in the jukebox, and lots of singles.

Front Page News
1104 Crescent Ave., Atlanta
(404) 897-3500 • www.fpnnews.com
Sit on the patio and relax in the warm outdoorsy atmosphere after visiting the make-your-own Bloody Mary bar featuring an enormous array of hot sauces, spices and mixers.

Chapter 4

The "It's Just Lunchbox" of Flirting Tips and Tools

Now that you're armed and ready with a great dating attitude, the lowdown on your options and places to go, it's time to get out and meet some people.

In this chapter we'll tackle the whole process from getting noticed to closing the deal in four simple steps.

Step 1: The Preliminaries

Rules of Attraction

Strike a Pose
Pause in the doorway with your head held high and shoulders back, and hold it there for a few seconds. The idea is to let all potential dates get a good look at you at your best. Then proceed across the room with confidence.

Divide and Conquer
Ladies: break up the pack. Men will never approach you when you are surrounded by your posse of girlfriends. And men, no woman in her right mind will stride up to a bunch of guys and shoulder her way through to you — no matter how cute you are. If you want to attract the opposite sex, make room for them to approach.

Smile
It lights up your face and will make you appear more friendly and open. If your attitude projects "speak to me at your own risk," people will stay away. Nobody likes rejection, so whoever appears most welcoming and approachable will be approached the most.

Use a Prop
What better way to bolster a conversation! Props come in

an infinite variety of packages, so carry one, wear one or bring one along at all times. For example, dogs are people magnets and natural-born flirts. Skilled at reading body language, they will walk right up to someone they're interested in and say hello (well sort of, since sniffing is basically the same thing), and they never take rejection personally.

Women can't resist a man with a small child. For some reason, many ladies believe that men who love children or animals are genuine sensitive types. A great prop for women is to wear something with a team logo. This never fails to attract men who love sports.

Another great flirting prop is a book — especially when the subject has a controversial or intriguing title. Hey, why not sit somewhere where you can be noticed and flash the cover of *this* book. That should get you some attention.

Step 2: The Approach

You spot someone across the room, your eyes lock, you feel a little giddy and there's a rush of blood to the head. Time to let them know you're interested, and at this stage of the game the eyes have it.

Close Encounters of the Opposite Sex Kind

Eye See You

The most effective flirting tools you have are your eyes. If you catch the eye of someone attractive, and they look back, don't become self-conscious and turn away. Women like men who are not afraid and know what they want, and men like women who give them clear signals. So be brave.

Do the glance — linger — look away — then reconnect routine. After a few times, the other person will know you're interested and will hopefully return the eye contact.

Guys, when you catch her eye on the reconnect, stay there until she looks away. Hold her gaze without giving her an *America's Most Wanted* stare, which means it's held just long enough to say, "I see you and I like you." Anything longer could scare her off. Then throw her a confident smile.

If a woman smiles at you a few times, this is your invitation to move in her direction. If you're up for it, go ahead. She could, of course, move over toward you, so smile and welcome her approach. Keep the eye-to-eye contact going and start putting those conversation skills to work.

Men Only
The Romantic Return

A friend of ours insists this trick always works: You spot a pretty woman across the room and you make eye contact for a while, but you're not completely convinced that she's interested in talking to Mr. Staring Guy. So you pay and leave without approaching her. Ten minutes later, you walk back in and stride right up to her and explain that "you just couldn't let this opportunity go by." Chances are you'll get her number. You see, leaving the scene and returning because you'll regret missing the chance takes you out of the lecherous category and puts you in the romantic fool category. It's so Hugh Grant, most women can't resist.

Instant Confidence

There they are, sitting at the end of the bar, looking great, looking out of your league. You approach, hoping you won't get blown off quickly. Stop right there! Try this quick psychological booster. Instead of thinking *what will they think of me?* turn it around to *will I like them?* Changing your thinking will adjust your body language and your conversation from timid to friendly and self-assured.

Feeling better? Okay, proceed to establishing contact.

You Had Them at Hello... Er — Maybe Not!

Walking up to a total stranger and starting a conversation can be terrifying, but if you don't learn to overcome your fear and wait for them to approach you first, you might end up waiting in the wings forever. Remember, they have the same fears and desires as you, so go ahead and take a few risks.

Yes, we know it's tough. Guys: She could totally ignore you and you'll have to quickly save face by pretending to speak with the person behind her. Or worse, ladies: He could laugh, then dismiss you with one of those looks of scorn, while all your friends gaze on. Oh, the humiliation!

Don't make it a big deal. If you don't get a favorable response, just say, "nice to meet you," and move on — no harm done. Not everyone is going to be intrigued, so don't try to force things or be too pushy — but know that most people are polite and the consequence of approaching someone is always worse in our minds than it is in real life.

Just be yourself, be friendly and smile. The confidence and warmth you exude when you approach someone will determine how successful you will be with your introduction. A sense of humor is always appreciated, but it's also important to be sincere.

Your goal is to generate good conversation, relate to people and get them interested — and to find out if you're interested in what they have to say. No matter how much you stumble or stammer in your initial approach, you will do 100% better than those who do nothing at all.

Avoid predictable opening lines like: "Where are you from?" OR "What do you do for a living?" OR "What do you do for fun?" Those questions are BORING!

Find questions that would engage *your* interest and go from there. There's no perfect opener, so trust your instincts and do what works best for you.

Observe first, so you can get some information to use as an opening line. For example, "Great party! Did you try those amazing apple martinis?" If they haven't, then offer to go with them and get one.

Or try a compliment: "I love your tie/jacket/ring." Then tell them why you like it, "It reminds me of..."

A great low-pressure conversation starter is to ask about someone else: "Do you know who that woman in the red dress is? She looks familiar."

In a class or a volunteer group, it's easier to find a subject to talk about. Steer the conversation toward something personal so you don't remain in neutral forever — like, "Great night! What inspired you to join (name of event or class)?" This way you move the conversation to a more emotional connection.

Confidence always gets the girl or boy, so if you don't let fear get in the way of romance, try this great icebreaker: *"It just occurred to me that a third person wasn't going to introduce us. Hi, my name is..."*

One last thought on opening lines — don't get too caught up in getting it right. When you get into a conversation with someone, unless you say something offensive right off the bat, you'll probably get to a few more sentences. Those are what will keep the conversation going.

All right! You've made contact. Now it's time to flirt.

Men Only
Rules of Attraction

Women know within the first few minutes of interacting with you whether or not you're a sexually confident man. It's all about your voice tone and body language. If you're not sure whether you project this "sexy beast" persona, chances are you don't. So, what's a guy to do? These four basic skills will instantly make you irresistible:

- **Lesson One:** Learn how to hold eye contact for longer than she does. Don't gawk, cold stare, or use darting eye glances. Just gently hold her gaze until she looks away. Avoiding eye contact reeks of emotional insecurity.

- **Lesson Two:** Women look first at your attire and second at how you hold yourself. Keep your body posture in a stance that says, "I'm the dominant male and I own this place." Suck in your stomach, hold your head up, chest out, shoulders back...and generally hold yourself like you're the most powerful person you've ever known. We know it seems a little awkward at first, but trust us, it'll work. Carry yourself like a manly man and women will have a positive subconscious, and then conscious, reaction to you.

- **Lesson Three:** Slow down. Confident people are not in a hurry. Fidgeting or nervous behavior shows insecurity and self-consciousness. Use slow, calculated gestures and movements. Walk slowly and with purpose, turn your head slowly, gesture slowly, even blink slowly. Emulate John Wayne or James Bond. This transmits a feeling of "I'm comfortable in my own skin," and makes a huge impact on women. Don't overdo it and become the slo-mo guy, but always project an attitude that you know what you're doing and where you're going.

continued on p. 39...

...continued from p. 38...

- **Lesson Four:** Lower your voice. A wobbly or high-pitched voice is a big turn-off for women since it relays low self-esteem. Moderately deep conveys confidence. Learn how to speak from the chest and stomach and not from the throat. Speak slower, articulate your words, pause more...it creates anticipation, which is sexy. If you talk too fast and too much when you get nervous, take a deep breath, let it out slowly, and relax. Stand up and hum a little before you leave a voicemail message—it will lower your pitch.

Step 3: The Flirt

It's Saturday night in a crowded bar. A man and woman are locked in conversation. She's laughing, batting her eyelashes and playing with her hair. He's standing with his head tilted slightly, leaning in toward her and occasionally touching her arm. They're performing a social ritual that's been around for more than 5,000 years — flirting.

Flirting is one of the great joys in life. It's an ego booster that makes you feel more attractive and desirable. Flirt with someone and they feel excited, flattered, appreciated and darn good about themselves. So indulge yourself whenever possible.

Two things are going on when you flirt. The first is the actual conversation, and the second is your body language. Flirting is an enticement and an invitation that lets the other person catch glimpses of your most attractive characteristics and behaviors. These days, it's a lost art, but it's great fun when done well.

Practice flirting with acquaintances or friends of the opposite sex (without telling them) and see what techniques get the best response.

For those who feel clueless about where to even start, we assure you that flirting is a learned behavior. It's not only possible to pick up the basics, but with a little practice, you can perfect the art. Let's start with the flirting conversation.

Can We Talk?

Flirting is considered a meta-conversation, which means

Women Only
Rules of Attraction

If you don't have the nerve to walk right up to a man and say hello, you could always bump into him... literally. That should get you noticed. Or ask for the time, a light, last week's notes, or where he got his jacket because you want to buy your brother one just like it. Even better: Ask for his advice. This makes him feel important and helpful — men love that. Ask him to explain something, give you directions or help you pick between two sweaters for your Dad. Get it? It doesn't matter what you say as long as it initiates a conversation.

it's three or four degrees of separation from what you're really saying. There's an underlying meaning to everything that's said. You might say directly, "That's really interesting," but the underlying meaning is, "I'm interested in you — perhaps sexually." There's a lot of unspoken communication going on: suggesting without stating, eye contact, body language, nods, smiles, encouragement and perhaps the start of something big.

Some men believe flirting is teasing encouragement and expect something at the end of it. If this is you, let us set you straight: *If a woman flirts with you, or you flirt with her, it's simply an opportunity for an entertaining exchange of playful banter. It doesn't mean you are guaranteed anything — not a dance, a drink, a date and especially not sex!*

Flirting is all about showing interest in the other person. So *ask questions and be attentive to the answers.*

Sometimes you can get caught up in the seductive aspect of flirting and find yourself stuck without a word to say. If this happens, there is a very powerful technique you can use called active listening. It's easy and will help you think of topics to discuss in any situation.

The most interesting people are usually the ones who are most interested in others. Suppose your date (or potential date) tells you about her day and she mentions that she bought plants for her garden. You can use that to move into a fun conversation.

Her garden might not mean anything to you, but it's obviously important to her. So you could say, "What's it like?" She'll jump at the chance to answer and actually think you're more interesting because you are interested in HER garden. And she'll become more interested in you!

A Few Conversation Dos

- Do be sincere. If her smile lights up the room, then tell her, but don't say something just for the sake of it. Insincere compliments are transparent.

- Do be yourself. Whatever's on your mind and in your heart will be the most natural thing you can talk about. Remember, they'll either like you or not. If they like you, great, if not... next! Why waste time trying to get someone's approval?

- Do be funny. Being light with a sense of humor helps people let their guard down, which could allow you more room to move in!

- Do say his or her name a few times; it'll make them feel special. But don't say it too much, or you'll sound like you just attended a cheesy sales seminar.

- Do keep it positive. Stick to your best attributes and the things you are most positive about. People become sexier as they talk excitedly and passionately about things that interest them.

- Do have fun with it. It's all about play!

A Few Conversation Don'ts

- Don't criticize personal choices, like wearing fur or who they voted for in the last election.

- Don't hog the conversation. It should flow back and forth like a tennis volley — you hit, he or she returns.

- Don't start talking about marriage or commitment on the first three dates.

- Don't use cheesy opening lines like, "Are you an Aquarius?"

Warning:
A Few Conversation Don'ts for Men
Avoid these danger zones!

- Don't corner her into revealing her age — it's never welcome.
- Don't use an authoritative or formal tone — save it for the office.
- Don't ask if she has kids right away. Single moms are sensitive about this and fear that you might have your "avoid the instant family" radar turned on.
- Don't compliment below the neck. No woman wants to know how you've checked out her nether regions.
- Don't go overboard with the bravado. Bragging about past conquests, thinking you know more about her anatomy/job/family than she does, or trying to impress her with your salary and net worth will leave you solo. Confidence is alluring — cockiness is not.
- Don't "over-friend." This means you're acting like all you want is to chat, because that's exactly what you'll end up with. Inject a little flirty banter into the conversation and don't hide your intentions.
- Don't "self reject." Deciding that someone is out of your league and failing to make a move will ensure you never get rejected or accepted. Why? Because you rejected yourself first!

The Language of Love
Want to know if that person you've been flirting with all night really likes you? Even if you're chatting about the weather, how people hold their bodies will tell you more than they want you to know.

Signals He Sends
- **The Grooming.** Adjusting or stroking his tie, fiddling with his collar or hand combing his hair.
- **The Loosening Off.** Partly unbuttoning his shirt or loosening his tie.
- **The Eyebrow Flash.** Raising his eyebrows and flashing them upward signals a strong interest.

Rules of Attraction

When couples are connecting deeply, they subconsciously mimic the other's body movements. If she leans forward, he'll likely do the same thing. If he touches his hair, she'll flip or stroke her own without even realizing it, and even blink rates and breathing will synchronize. It's fun to watch. Check out couples that are locked in seduction mode next time you're in a restaurant or bar setting.

- **The Arm Guide.** Walking you through a room with his arm around the small of your back or holding your elbow.
- **The Head Tilt.** Standing with his head cocked slightly to one side.
- **The Walk.** It becomes strong and determined — he knows where he's going.

Signals She Sends

- **The Smiles.** Lots of them. If she laughs at your jokes too, she really likes you.
- **The Eye Linger.** Holding your gaze signals a strong sexual interest.
- **The Lip Lick.** Licking or biting her lips or running her tongue across her front teeth draws your attention to her mouth and is intriguing.
- **The Touch and the Lean.** Leaning forward and touching your arm is her way of bestowing affection on you — she's inviting you into her personal space.
- **The Fondle.** Plays with her jewelry, especially with stroking and pulling motions.
- **The Kick and Thrust.** Crossing one leg over the other and pointing it toward you or kicking it out and up while thrusting her body forward.

Signals You Both Send

- Accidental touches
- Leaning forward
- Eye contact
- Smiles
- Open body position

Road-Tested Flirting Techniques

Being a skillful flirt is all about using the correct body language and the right amount of attitude. Here are 10 steps to help you perfect the art of flirting.

- **Make meaningful eye contact and smile.** Let your eyes linger on his or her eyes while you're talking, then smile immediately when you feel a connection.

- **Get interested in them and they'll get interested in you.** What is it that people like to talk about most? Themselves, of course. Ask questions about where they like to go, what they like to do, who interests them, and why they do what they do, and you'll be talking all night.

- **Deliver a compliment.** Flattery may not get you everywhere, but it does open doors. Keep it sincere.

- **Listen attentively.** Being a good listener is a potent aphrodisiac.

- **Tell it like it is.** Being vulnerable and honest is the slam-dunk, sexiest thing a man or woman can be. Getting "real" with someone is not only easier than the pretense most people create, it also saves you unnecessary angst in the long run. Just don't get too personal, too soon.

- **Be enthusiastic.** As a flirt, you want the person you're flirting with to feel good about you and to experience you as a fun, happy, great-to-be-with person. If you feel that you are, it shows. If you sit next to them thinking, *I'm having fun, this is great, I'm so glad to be here,* it really comes across to the other person.

- **Draw them in.** Lean forward, not because you want to show off your cleavage or your muscles, but to convey interest. Talk to them actively, showing that you like them. Then start talking more quietly and intimately. They'll need to get closer to hear you so draw them in with your voice. Guys, gauge her "personal zone" and then encroach on it just an inch. Leaning in too far can seem too forceful.

- **Touch him or her.** The sense of touch heightens during flirting and can actually send tingles through a person's body. Realize this power and watch for ways to use it. Once you've become comfortable, lightly brush shoulders, or touch their hand or arm if they say something funny. This can work wonders if the signals are there.

Step 4: The Proposition

You've spent the entire evening flirting with a total dream. You're on fire, loving life, feeling wanted and bursting to know if they share your feelings. She (or he) hasn't made any moves to leave and scope out other prospects. The best way to find out is by going on a date.

What's stopping you?

Oh... you have to ask first.

You may yet be rejected, but if you don't make a move, they might never know how you feel. What's worse, someone else might take the plunge first and you know you'll hate yourself if that happens.

It's a dilemma. So, what should you do? You can start by briefing yourself on the following tips for popping the question:

What to Say

First, relax. Try not to view it as a date, look at asking her out as an invitation instead. Better still — take the pressure off by not using the "D" word altogether. Don't ask for a date and don't call it a date. It starts to get significant when that word appears, so focus on the activity and position it in the same informal way you would ask a friend.

Keep the invitation light and casual. The whole reason *It's Just Lunch* is the success it is today, arranging more than 50,000 first dates each month, is because we do just that.

A lunch date is low pressure — it has a beginning and an end, and both occur within an hour or so. It's easy to say goodbye, there's no goodnight kiss, no obligation, and so the pressure is off.

If you're dating through *It's Just Lunch*, we do the first-date asking for you, so it's really easy. But if you want to ask for a second date or if you're going it alone from the start, there are a few things to keep in mind when asking someone out.

Here's What *Not* to Say

- Don't ask, "You want to go out sometime?" It's too

open-ended and can lead to an awkward follow-up conversation.

- Don't ask, "What are you doing Friday night?" It's too vague and it might leave your potential date wondering if you're just curious about what he or she is doing on Friday night, or if you want to do something together.

- Don't use a sexually suggestive line like, "I'd love to have breakfast with you. Should I call you or nudge you?" It might be funny if you read it in a book, but in the real world, it's liable to get you a speedy rejection. These types of lines don't show that you're genuinely interested in a person — they make you seem a little too slick.

What Works Best?

Before you ask, consider the following:

- **Be a friend first, not a potential date.** If you really want to get to know someone better, the key is to relax and allow your own personality to shine through. There really is no need to be a smart-ass, or make them laugh out loud. You just need to be good company, because the more comfortable you both feel, the easier it is to recognize any chemistry between you. In short, forget the pickup lines. Show an interest in them, and they will only be flattered.

- **Create an opportunity for your date.** Once you know more about what that person likes to do, you can offer something. After all, a date is an invitation. If they love art, ask them to the latest big museum exhibition; if they like sports, offer tickets to a basketball game. If they enjoy wine, ask them to a wine tasting.

- **Drop a hint.** Ask about a subject and drop a hint. Say something like, "What do you like to do on the weekends?" As she responds, look for something you like to do too. If she says she loves to hike, respond with, "We should go hiking together sometime," then move on in the conversation and ask about her favorite hiking spots.

The Business Card

Handing someone your card is a less threatening way of putting the ball in their court. If you find you're just too shy to go over and strike up a conversation, or perhaps you're in a noisy location, which makes it difficult to break the ice, then make sure you carry a few extra business cards around with you. Write a short note on the back. Say something like, "The noise makes it difficult to talk, but I'd really like to meet you. You can reach me at _____." Or if you're shy, say, "I think you're really attractive but I'm a little shy. If you'd like to talk sometime please call me on _____."

You've just dropped a big hint, so let it sink in for a while. Listen carefully to her response and gauge her enthusiasm. If she stays upbeat and positive, ask her if she would like to go hiking with you next weekend.

- **Keep it casual.** If you feel uncomfortable saying, "Would you like to go to dinner Friday night?" try something like this:

  "I was thinking about going for a ride along the boardwalk on Sunday. It's going to be a beautiful day. Would you like to go with me?" Pose the question as if you're already going and they can join you, if interested. This will make you feel less desperate and take the pressure off them if they say no.

- **Be specific when asking for the date.** "I'd like to take you for coffee this Thursday" is more powerful than asking if she'd like to "go out sometime."

  Of course, you could always invite the person on a group date, since that really takes the pressure off. Invite them bowling, to play volleyball, or to join a bunch of friends for a drink or to a party. As soon as you say, "A bunch of us are going to..." it takes the pressure off. "Us" is the operative word here.

  Read the situation. If you've hung out for a while and all the signs suggest your potential date shares your feelings, then either a) you won't be able to keep your hands off each other, or b) you'll be able to suggest meeting up for an evening out knowing that's what they want too! If that vibe isn't happening, at the very least you'll have made a new friend.

So remember, when you are asking someone out, *plan ahead* and *be specific*. Know what you are going to say AND what you want to suggest doing on the date.

Your prospective dates will be much more comfortable if they know exactly what you want to do.

Just try to relax and enjoy yourself. Worst case scenario — they'll say they can't go out. And that will bring you one step closer to someone who can. Someone who appreciates you and where the chemistry connection is reciprocated and the sparks really fly. Let's face it, getting to that special someone inevitably means dealing with a few duds along the way. It'll be worth it in the end.

Should She Ask?

Absolutely! It's no longer fashionable to leave it up to the man. Most men will be flattered, impressed, and relieved if you have the courage to ask them out. These days, men appreciate women who take the initiative and go after what they want in life. Guys find confident women extremely sexy. It may seem hard to initiate a request for a date if you're not used to it, but do it a few times and it'll become a piece of cake.

Getting a No or Saying No

Dating is a numbers game. You may have several misses before you get a hit. Don't take it personally or assume you did something wrong. View each rejection as bringing you one step closer to your ideal mate.

If you're the one who isn't interested, most of all, be kind. Say something nice about them and then end it with a, "no, thank you."

Try not to be overly sensitive to rejection or get overly emotionally invested with the other person too soon. Either makes a rebuff become equally, if not more, painful. Simply move on!

The Lists

Three Best Flirting Hotspots

Four Seasons Hotel
75 14th St., N.E., Atlanta
(404) 253-3800 • www.fourseasons.com

The lounge at the *Four Seasons Hotel* gives new meaning to swank. Cloth napkins and homemade potato chips add that certain je ne sais quoi, don't you think?

Ritz-Carlton Buckhead
3434 Peachtree Rd. N.E., Atlanta
(404) 237-2700 • www.ritzcarlton.com

Sipping a Cosmo in the bar at the *Ritz-Carlton Buckhead* is sheer elegance. You'll feel like a billionaire.

Bone's Restaurant
3130 Piedmont Rd. N.E., Atlanta
(404) 237-2663 • www.bonesrestaurant.com

Join successful business-types for an after-work drink and wind down for the day. *Bone's* is especially popular with the Buckhead crowd.

Five Best Places To Flirt With Rhythm (Live Music Venues)

The Tabernacle
152 Luckie St. N.W., Atlanta
(404) 659-9022

This venue is a favorite with die-hard blues fans, and its rich character makes any show memorable. Sit and listen or hit the dance flooræthere's a great view from every angle.

Churchill Grounds
660 Peachtree St. N.E., Atlanta
(404) 876-3030

Conveniently located between midtown and downtown, this jazz club offers a romantic and comfortable ambiance. For a laugh, check out Tuesday night improv.

Chastain Park Amphitheater
4469 Stella Dr., Atlanta
(404) 233-2227

A popular outdoor summer venue hosting "oldies, but

---

goodies" like Tony Bennett, the Moody Blues and James
Taylor. Share a picnic, a bottle of wine, and enjoy the
scenery.

Philips Arena
190 Marietta St. N., Atlanta
(404) 827-3000 • www.phillipsarena.com

This state-of-the-art arena attracts sporting events and top
names in music like Usher, Avril Lavine, and Annie Lennox.
With the jumbo screens, every seat has a great view.

Lakewood Amphitheater
2002 Lakewood Ave. S.W., Atlanta
(404) 627-9704

Another summertime favorite for big name acts. Seating is
available close to the stage, but regular concert goers seem
to prefer the lawn seating.

Chapter 5

It's a Date!

Alright! You've got a date. You mustered up the courage to suggest a get-together and got a "yes." Don't you feel good? Yes... No? Well, chances are you could be slightly delirious at this point. It's perfectly natural to be nervous about looking good or anticipating that first kiss. Then there's the possibility of finding true love; one thing could lead to another and before you know it — enough! Stay grounded but enthusiastic.

There are two things you need to decide right now: What to do on your date (if you did the asking), and what to wear.

Where to Go

Figuring out the best place to go on a first date can be a bit daunting. If you're an *It's Just Lunch* member we set up the first date for you. We pick the restaurant, we make the reservation and arrangements with your date, and all you need to do is show up. Easy stuff!

If you're arranging the date yourself, you may think that you should do something impressive or unique. But in our experience — and that would be more than two million first dates — simple and casual is always better when you're meeting someone for the first time. Choose a place where you feel comfortable and familiar, so you don't waste time trying to figure out the lay of the land or that 20-page Japanese menu. This way, you can relax and focus on your date.

The purpose of a first date is to get to know each other better, so it's important to find a venue that isn't too distracting or too loud — somewhere you can have a nice, cozy chat without trying to outrap the sound system.

Lunch or Coffee Date

If it's a blind date or you're not sure how you feel about the person, keep it low pressure and go for coffee, lunch, or brunch. If you meet for lunch, you can use the excuse of having to get back to work if the date is a flop. And if it's fun, you can arrange to meet again and do something more exciting.

After-Work Drinks

This is another low-commitment, low-cost date that will allow you the option of continuing with dinner if things go well. Or you can call it a night after one drink — say you've got dinner plans elsewhere or you need to get an early start in the morning. Word to the wise: Alcohol on an empty stomach can cloud your judgment, so stick to one or two drinks.

Drinks and Dinner

Going out for dinner is a popular option for a first date, but one we don't recommend, especially if you don't know the person at all. Dinner puts you on the spot. If the two of you don't really "click," you're forced to sit and face each other while making polite chitchat.

Dress to Impress

Once you've agreed on a time and place for your date, it's time to figure out what to wear.

Though clothes can never be a substitute for self-confidence or a positive attitude, they can go a long way in making a good impression and give you a head start on landing a second date.

What's most important about dressing for a first date is wearing something that you feel comfortable in, both physically and mentally. Just reach for your favorite confidence-boosting outfit that makes you feel like a million bucks.

Keep It Simple

Fashion-wise, what works best for a first date? Obviously, tastes vary, but you'll come out a winner if you remember that less is more. Keep your overall style simple and stay away from anything extreme.

For example, don't choose really tight pants or extra baggy ones — wear something more classic. Once you get to know the other person better, you can start injecting the pieces that better reflect your personality.

Leave Some Things to the Imagination

Stay away from clothes that are too tight or revealing — even if you have a killer body. Let your date wonder what you look like under that shirt or sweater.

There's nothing wrong with wearing something fitted that emphasizes your physique — after all, you worked hard for it — but make sure you don't resemble an over-stuffed turkey. On the other hand, if you're less buff and/or a little heavy, wear something to camouflage any problem areas.

Get Some Advice

If you're still having difficulty knowing what looks best on you, ask someone with a good sense of style for help. This someone should give you *honest* feedback, since it's not going to help if he or she insists you look great in everything. Go through your wardrobe and put together six outfits that look good on you, each one right for a different type of event, and then make the final decision.

Pick out clothes that make you feel attractive and confident, that best represent your personality and style, that aren't too over the top or make you look like you're trying too hard. You want to appear secure and relaxed.

Men Only

If you want to put a little distance between you and the average Joe, who frankly, isn't looking so stylish these days, a few simple fashion rules ensure great style and keep you ahead of the game.

- **Keep your colors to a minimum and work mostly with neutrals.** We're talking black, gray, navy, white or beige. And if you wear a black sweater, make sure you have a black belt and black shoes. That way, if your pants are a different color, you'll have a total of two colors.

   Stylish shoes are a must on your first date because women believe shoes reveal a lot about your personality, and they also complete your overall look. Make sure they're clean and polished — women notice this stuff and scuffed shoes look unkempt.

- **Keep accessories to a minimum too.** A watch is the only piece of jewelry any man really needs, and women know that a timepiece, like shoes, says a lot about a man. This is the one item you should invest in. It's better to have one good watch than several mediocre ones. If you're limited to one watch, make sure it can move easily from casual to dressy.

   If you must add additional jewelry, limit it to a

ring or a simple chain around the neck. The whole point of keeping it low key is so your date doesn't spend the night focusing on your "bling," but has her attention turned toward you.

Polishing Your Image

Now that you've got your ensemble figured out, let's move on to the grooming. Even if you're as handsome as George Clooney or Tom Cruise, it's important to look and smell your best when you're trying to impress a woman for the first time. Follow these guidelines to make sure all your angles are covered:

1. **Wash hair:** Definitely shampoo on the day you expect to meet up with your date. If your hair isn't clean, she will definitely notice. This is one of the most important criteria she'll judge you on, so make sure your hair is clean.

2. **Polish your face:** Wash your face and shave. Always shave in the direction your hair grows. If you go against the grain it can cause razor burn. *You'll score extra points with a woman if you moisturize your skin before you shave* — moist skin looks better than a scaly face.

3. **Clean and trim nails:** Dirty, messy nails are the number one turnoff for women. Put yourself in her shoes. How excited would you be to have some guy's grubby fingers all over you?

4. **Check Nose and Ears:** Make sure you possess and regularly use those simple but ingenious devices, the Q-tip and the nose-hair trimmer.

5. **Apply deodorant and cologne:** Don't forget to rub on plenty of underarm deodorant before you head out on that date. Damp armpits are obviously very high on the list of turnoffs.

   Here's something you might not know: Spraying on the right cologne could put her in the mood for love. Researchers have found that Oriental blends of spicy notes like ambergris, cinnamon and vanilla with sultry, animal odors like musk — are the perfume world's aphrodisiacs with warm, intoxicating qualities. In studies, the scent of pumpkin pie (which contains the same sweet and spicy notes) caused more sexual arousal than any other scent. But when it comes to cologne, remember less is more, so don't overdo it — and the same applies to pumpkin pie.

6. **Freshen breath:** Fresh breath is a must-have in any dating situation, especially so when it's time to deliver your first kiss. Make sure you brush and floss regularly, and keep plenty of breath mints, spray or gum at hand.

Piece of cake right? Now have a splendid first date.

Women Only: She's Gotta Have It

The right clothing might not change your life, but it can change your mood for the better. And while we always say that confidence is the sexiest thing you can wear on a first date, there are specific items that look great on every woman and will go a long way in making you feel extra flirty.

For starters, every woman should wear more cashmere. It not only feels good on your skin, it holds the curves of a woman without being too obvious. A snug three-quarter-sleeve sweater is an item every woman should have in her closet.

Of course he'll want to touch it too — no one can resist the feel of cashmere, so be prepared.

Anything made from silk charmeuse or satin, such as a bias-cut skirt, fitted blouse, scoop or V-neck top or camisole will work wonders for your sex appeal. Silk or satin tops are perfectly paired with fitted jeans. Skirts should be worn with a finely knit sweater or silk jersey top.

And don't forget the high heels. Platforms and wedges don't count. Guys love gals in sky-high heels.

Style Secrets

When you put your outfit together, start with a piece that you love and build the rest of the look around that. Never wear one designer outfit from head to toe — instead, mix high with low to create your own signature style.

Accessories can seal the deal when it comes to stylish dressing, but don't overdo it. Keep jewelry to a minimum. If you're wearing a low-cut top, pair it with a simple necklace and one statement ring, or do the earrings-bracelet approach. But never mix all four pieces.

Evocation, not Provocation

Flaunting your assets may show that you have no inhibitions, but it also shows a lack of self-confidence — like you need to be reassured of your beauty and sex appeal. Discretion is now the better part of sex appeal. Shoot for evocative — it's what he doesn't see but can imagine that's really titillating. A hint of gold-dusted cleavage; a skirt that stops at the knee revealing smooth, shimmery legs; pants that fit like a second skin, not tighter than your first; and floaty or sensual fabrics. These all say sexy, not smutty.

Accentuate the Positive

Pick your best feature and show it off. Great legs? Choose an above-the-knee skirt. Nice curves? Try a form-fitting dress. Great cleavage? Small waist? A wrap top will accentuate both. Whether you're a few pounds overweight or a skinny stick, there's something about you that *is* great and the world needs to know about it. If you can't figure it out, ask a friend.

Hair and Makeup from a Man's Perspective

A lot of men we talk to prefer women who wear little to no makeup and have that natural, un-fussed look. We agree! Flushed, dewy skin; moist, juicy lips; tousled hair — it's all so straight-from-the-bedroom sexy. Little do they know this can take a heck of a lot more time to create than slapping on the eye shadow and mascara Tammy Faye style.

Some guys appreciate a touch of drama like a smoky eye or a scarlet lip on the right occasion. If you decide to crank up the pace, a black eye pencil transforms a nicely natural face into a stylishly sexy one. Or go with a stronger lip and apply a classic red lipstick, but keep the rest of your makeup natural and neutral. One bold statement on the face is enough.

We suggest you keep makeup to a minimum and focus on your lips and hair, fuller and glossier for both. Also, now is not the time to try a new look, unless you've tried it before and know it looks good. You want to feel confident, so stick with colors you normally wear.

Showing off the décolletage area is flattering on most women at any age. The skin is extremely pretty there, as it hasn't had as much sun exposure. Add extra gleam to your skin with a light dusting of reflective gold powder along the collarbones. To make lips look fuller (and more kissable), apply a dab of shimmery lipgloss to the center of your bottom lip. Simply irresistible!

Get Your Own Make-Over

From *Queer Eye for the Straight Guy* to *Extreme Makeover*, everybody's indulging in a little body change madness these days — and why not? It makes you look and feel like a million dollars.

Most upscale hair salons provide makeup services, and they even offer lessons for those who would like to try a new look but are unsure where to start.

Why not stop by the cosmetics counter at your favorite department store and get a free makeover? You'll have to purchase a few of the recommended products, but it's well worth it.

A word of warning: Some sales associates can be a little heavy handed with the colors, so make sure you tell them that you prefer natural shades and don't want to look overdone. The best places to get a minimal makeup look are Laura Mercier, Clinique and Bobbi Brown.

Hot Heads

Ever since Rapunzel let down her long locks, gorgeous hair has ranked high on most men's lists of fetching female attributes. Whether you opt for long or short, straight or wavy, up or down, sexy hair must have two qualities: It has to be touchable and it has to smell good. Devote time to your tresses before your date.

Sexy hair is hair that doesn't look *done*, where he can actually run his fingers through it. Stay away from the hairspray. Instead, opt for a glossing balm to tame the frizzies and give you a super-smooth texture — a little goes a long way and it'll restore your luster. He'll long to reach out and touch.

Although many men say they love long hair, short styles can be incredibly sexy because they expose the neck. If you have good cheekbones and a small face, short hair looks extremely feminine — think Halle Berry, Ashley Judd or Sharon Stone.

The Lists

Five Best Places to Relax before a Date

Studio Oliver Salon
789 Argonne Ave. N.E., Atlanta
(404) 607-9757 • www.studiooliver.com
One of Atlanta's best salons in the heart of midtown. Prices
are what you'd expect to pay for great service and products
like *Bumble & Bumble, Kerastase,* and *Mario Badescu.*

Key Lime Pie Salon
806 N Highland Ave. N.E., Atlanta
(404) 873-6512 • www.keylimepie.net
Its professional, down-to-earth staff and full-service salon
and spa menu make this cozy hideaway a favorite stop for
Atlanta's beautiful people.

Aruka Salon
555 S. Atlanta St. Ste. A400, Roswell
(770) 993-0322
Delicious *Aveda* products and a super-friendly staff create
calm from the moment you arrive. Quiet and elegant, this
full-service salon and spa will suit you to a tee.

Sweetgrass Wellness Spring
483 Moreland Ave. N.E., Atlanta
(404) 522-3223 • www.sweetgrasswellness.com
Visit this spa featuring only organic products to help
soothe your mind and relax your body before the big date.

Wolf Creek Golf Club
3000 Union Rd. S.W., Atlanta
(404) 344-1334 • www.wolfcreekgc.com
Grab your favorite driver and relax before your night out
by pounding out a bucket of balls—or two. Golf is also a
great workout for those forearms.

Five Best Places to Put You in a Dating Mood

Strings n' Strands
4632 Weiuca Rd., Atlanta
(404) 252-9662
Hey, why not? Knitting is all the rage these days. This yarn

boutique has the latest trends and fashions. So take a class—or just pick up a one-of-a-kind scarf to wear on your date.

Nicholas Kniel Embellishments
290 Hilderbrand Dr. N.E., Atlanta
(404) 252-8855

Love this place! It has the best funky accents to make any outfit a standout—everything from vintage couture beads to ribbons, trims, and brooches. Go ahead—accessorize!

Intimacy
3500 Peachtree Rd. N.E., Atlanta
(404) 261-9333 • www.intimacyofatlanta.com

With some of the finest lingerie in Atlanta, this upscale boutique offers custom fitting and tailoring of lingerie/swimsuits, specializing in upscale labels like *Felina* and *La Perla*.

L'Occitane
4400 Ashford Dunwoody Rd. NE, Atlanta
(678) 441-0515
Other locations: Peachtree Rd. and Alpharetta
www.loccitane.com

Would a nice relaxing bath put you in a great mood for your date? Then *L'Occitane* is the place for you! Their scented products are just yummy.

Miracles of Massage
4790 Sugarloaf Pkwy., Ste. 100, Lawrenceville
(770) 366-9438

Put yourself in expert hands—literally—and you'll be perfect and purring before your night on the town.

Chapter 6

The First Date

Congratulations, you're officially dating!

However, if a little voice inside your head is trying to talk you out of it, don't panic. A little nervousness is perfectly natural.

Yes, it's true that dating means taking risks. Heaven forbid, you might get dumped. But the good news is, *you'll live*. The happiest people are those willing to step outside their comfort zones and take a few risks, because the potential for rewards is so great.

As for rejection, don't take it personally. It's just part of the dating journey. It will lead to bigger and better things — and eventually a few laughs as well.

Here's the key: Learn how to distinguish between describing the date as a failure and seeing *yourself* as a failure. It's not the same thing. Not everyone will be a match. And how else are you going to find the person who's right for you?

Every date is a learning opportunity — a chance to observe yourself. So there's really nothing to be nervous about. Treat dating as an adventure. Take it lightly and it can be fun.

Most of all, you'll be really, *really* living life to the max. Now what's so bad about that?

Safety First

Okay, we know this subject is not romantic, but it's necessary! Before you set out on your first date, there are a couple of safety measures you need to take so you can rest assured that even if you end up lunching with a Ted Bundy type, you'll be around to talk about it later.

Guys, this applies to you too. Before you groan, laugh or throw this book away in total disgust, we have five words for you: Glenn Close in *Fatal Attraction*. Convinced?

If it's an *It's Just Lunch* date, then you can rest assured that we've done our absolute best to pair you up with someone of sound mind. But we're not Big Brother, so use your best judgment when meeting someone the first few times. Our dates are set up with safety and discretion in mind. We work with both of you directly to arrange a time and place for you to meet, and we never give out any of your personal information.

If you're going it alone and meeting someone you've never met before (blind date, Internet date, someone you met in a bar) versus someone you've known for a while or who has been recommended by a mutual friend, then do the following:

- Arrange to meet your date in a public place like a restaurant or bar.
- Don't let them change the location at the last minute.
- Give out your cell phone number rather than home phone.
- Let friends know the details of your date and when you expect to be home.
- Don't get in a car with him or her.
- Trust your instincts. If you find yourself in a situation that makes you feel uncomfortable, leave.
- Don't hesitate to leave if your new date shows signs of drunkenness, rage, hysteria, rudeness, disrespect, recklessness or any other embarrassing or dangerous behavior.

What to Expect

A first date is all about getting to know the other person a little better and walking away with a sense of whether or not you want to see them again. *Stop right there!* That's all there is to it.

Don't go on a first date with an agenda or a checklist of non-negotiables. There will be subsequent dates to find out if he's open to having kids, or her views on the last election or his sexual history.

Keep It in perspective

Try to keep it light and fun. Don't lose sight of the fact that *it's just a date!*

Marriage should not be the goal (or the topic of conversation). You have no idea how it will turn out and have no control over that anyway. It will either work or it won't. So relax, laugh at yourself if you notice you're getting a little absurd (like thinking about picking out your china pattern together) or making the date too significant.

Pay attention to what you are learning about your date. No matter how excited, thrilled or turned on you might

79% of men on a first date take 15 minutes to determine whether or not they want to see a woman again.

be, it's important to listen. Otherwise, you can go through the whole date in a giddy daze and not remember anything later.

Enjoy Yourself
Focus on being pleasant and having fun. And don't forget to smile. It makes you more attractive. And who knows, you might have a good time. You might even meet the love of your life!

Women Only

What Men Look for in a First Date
As much as some of us would like to believe that men are above judging a woman based on her looks, it's simply not true. (Actually, women do it too.) Men are very visual beings, and sexual attraction ranks highest on their list. The good news is that our national surveys show that looks are not the only attribute men look for; qualities like intelligence and a sense of humor are equally important.

So what really attracts men? Most men are attracted to women who are intelligent, witty, passionate, confident and who are good conversationalists.

What Turns Men On?
Eye contact — men love flirty eyes and lots of smiles. They like it when you focus your attention on them and are genuinely interested in getting to know them better. Men also love women who appreciate humor.

What Turns Men Off?
Being drunk, negative conversation, complaints, self-pity and not laughing at their jokes.

Men Only

What Women Look for in a First Date
Self-confidence is extremely sexy to a woman. In fact, we'd go as far as to say that, more than a man's looks, job status or good manners, confidence is a winning trait that gets the girl. As old-fashioned as it might sound, women want

What Men Look for on a First Date

Through the years we've talked with thousands of men about what they look for in a first date. A 38-year-old CEO gave us this checklist, which pretty much sums it up.

- Does she complain about men?
- Is she open to trying new things?
- Do I like her clothes and sense of style?
- Can she speak intelligently about more than one thing (such as her job)?
- Is she emotionally available or is she still talking to her ex a lot? *(This is very important!)*
- Can she maintain eye contact? Is she nervous? Is there some energy between us or is it flat? (Nervous is better than flat.)
- Is she generous or is she confrontational? Can she hold her own opinion without making me wrong?
- Does she have a good sense of humor and a "fun" attitude? Does she get my sense of humor? Is she happy?
- Do we have chemistry? How does she respond when I put my hand on the side of her arm or in the small of her back? Is she open and not afraid to show that she likes me?
- Is she high maintenance? Does she talk about nicer places than the one you are taking her to in a way that makes you think she would have rather gone there? Does she pick the most expensive thing on the menu on the first date?

someone who's not going to run from a fight; a man who is confident in his ability to provide and protect. Women also like men who aren't afraid of emotional intimacy, who can talk openly and are willing to share their thoughts and feelings. Our research shows that the top three qualities women seek in a man are good communication skills, intelligence and a sense of humor.

What Turns Women On?

Chivalry is not dead. Good manners (holding the door open, pulling out the chair and helping with her coat) are still attractive to women. Lots of eye contact, attentiveness and being a good listener are other traits women appreciate.

What Women Look for on a First Date

Wondering what really scores high with women? Here's a checklist we gathered from a number of women that may give you some insight:

- Does he carry himself with confidence?
- Did he complain about every aspect of his life?
- Does he appear trustworthy, dependable and honest?
- Do we have good chemistry? Am I attracted to him?
- Do I like his sense of humor? Does he have one? Did we have fun together?
- Was he complimentary? Did he say something positive about the way I look?
- Did he only have eyes for me? Or was he interested in other women in the room?
- Is he a good communicator? Did he listen and appear to be interested in what I had to say?
- Is he well groomed with good hygiene? Clothes clean and pressed?
- Is he interesting? Did we engage easily in conversation or was it a struggle? Did he only talk about himself?
- Is he intelligent? Does he seem interested in life? Is he the type of man who makes things happen?
- Does he have good manners? Did he show me consideration and treat me with respect? Is he polite to others? Was he insulting about his exes?

What Turns Women Off?

Unsolicited sexual advances. Bragging about past conquests. Checking out other women. Constantly talking about yourself and not listening to her. Calling her "babe" on the first date. Bad hygiene. Bad attitude. Bad manners!

Conversation Starters

It always helps to have a couple of topics in mind or a few questions handy should your conversation ever fall into one of those awkward silences. If that happens, don't start squirming in your seat and getting all self-conscious and weird. It's perfectly normal to fall into the occasional lull.

64% of women will take an hour on a first date to determine if they would see a man again.

In fact, it's a great icebreaker if you just acknowledge it by saying something like, "Are we having one of those weird silent moments?" Seriously, your date will probably laugh and that will put you both at ease.

Need a little help with some clever conversation? Check out these great starters:

- Find out what they like to do in their free time.
- Talk about your travel experiences — trips you've been on or places you'd like to visit and why.
- Mention current events or news. Ask your dates what they think about a topic.
- Talk about where you grew up, your family, then ask about theirs.
- Ask about their favorite sports teams, movies, plays and books.
- Talk about something exciting in your life. A high school reunion, a promotion, a new home.
- Notice something positive about your date (nice hair, eyes, an expression or gesture) and compliment them on it.
- Ask a fun question like, "If you could change places with anyone in the world, living or dead, who would it be?"
- Mention something beautiful or touching you've seen or experienced in the past week. Even if it was just in a movie!
- Talk about the things you're most passionate about, from volunteering at a homeless shelter to your 1980s record collection.
- Ask about their dreams for the future. This will get them excited. (*But please don't turn this into a deal breaker.*)

Conversation Killers

Try not to say things just to please or impress and stay away from sensitive or taboo subjects such as religion or politics — at least on the first few dates.

Avoid talking about the following:

- Ex-anything. Leave your past relationships in the past for the first date.
- Other people you're dating.

5 Talkin' Tips

1. Keep up with current events so you can talk intelligently about major developments.
2. When you talk about yourself, keep it positive. Stick to your best attributes and the interests you're most passionate about.
3. Ask open-ended question's that evoke a response beyond yes or no.
4. Practice listening. You could do this with a friend. Have them read you a story from the paper and see how much you remember.
5. Try learning five jokes that are clean and not demeaning to anyone. This may take a while, but it's actually a useful "tool" in many situations.

- Personal topics like cosmetic surgery, medical history or "if only I could lose 10 lbs."
- Marriage, or your plans for a large family.
- Superficial things such as an interest in money or that sexy little Porsche you just bought.
- How much you pay (or get) in alimony.
- Controversial political topics: capital punishment, abortion, and your cousin's gay rights — these topics are better left for a later date.
- Name dropping, bragging or showing off in general.

Who Pays?

If you're on an *It's Just Lunch* first date, it's our policy that you split the check. It's just easier that way and takes away the whole "who pays" dilemma. On subsequent dates we suggest the following:

- Whoever does the asking should pay for the date. If he asks you out to dinner, he picks up the check. If she asks you to the symphony, she gets the tickets.
- If one person makes significantly more money than the other, then he or she could carry the majority of the weight, but the other person can contribute by paying for less expensive dates or making dinner on a romantic night in.
- No matter who pays, it's generally a nice gesture for the other person to offer to contribute (if you have been dating for a while).

Visitors surveyed on our website say that these are the four worst conversation killers: past relationships—49%, dieting or body image—21%, politics—15% and marriage—15%.

Most Common Dating Mistakes

Oh, c'mon. We've all made them. Confession is good for the soul. Take a look at "Most Common Dating Mistakes" on page 69 to see how your mistakes compare to our national singles survey. Then we'll look at them one at a time.

Judging Your Date

Picture this. You're sitting at the table waiting for your date to arrive. He or she comes in, walks up to the table and says, "Hi." Do you respond by saying, a) "Pardon, you must have the wrong person," then grab your coat and leave or, b) "Take a seat, I've been looking forward to meeting you?" Tell the truth! Many people make the mistake of immediately judging their dates negatively and don't even give them a chance.

If you catch yourself stacking up hurdles in front of your potential love matches, chances are none of them will make it to the finish line.

Unrealistic Expectations

This one happens a lot. We get so excited about the fantasy of our date that we start imagining all sorts of unrealistic ideals. By the time we get there we're expecting to have lunch with George Clooney or Angelina Jolie. No wonder it's a letdown!

Get rid of all your expectations on a first date. This is not the time to decide whether or not he or she meets your criteria for everlasting love. *It's just a date!*

Not Paying Attention

So by now we know that the most important part of a first date is to get to know the other person a little better, right? Well, you'd think so. But what often happens is that we spend too much time in our own head preoccupied with our own thoughts about what our date thinks about us.

If you're wondering whether or not you are doing the right thing, if you look good in that light, or if she can see your bald spot, you're going to miss out on the actual date.

5 Questions You Should Never Ask Your Date

1. Do I look fat?
2. What did you look like with hair?
3. How many lovers have you had?
4. How much can a partner at your law firm expect to make?
5. What is your ex like?

If your mind isn't focused on your date, how can your date get a sense of who you really are? And how will you know anything about him or her when you've spent most of the date worrying about yourself?

It's impossible to know for sure if your date likes you or not (unless they tell you), so give it up!

Not Listening and Talking Too Much

These two usually go hand in hand. It's really important to be able to listen to the other person, and that doesn't just mean letting them speak, but also not trying to figure out what you're going to say while they're speaking. There's no way you can listen and think of a smart response at the same time.

Rambling on or talking "at" someone kills the experience of communication and alienates people. It's a big turnoff.

Your aim is to learn about your date; so ask questions, listen and let them do roughly 50 percent of the talking.

First Date Dos

When it's time to go on your first date, don't forget the basics:

- DO smile. Smile a lot. You'll feel better.
- DO have fun. Remember, *it's just a date!*
- DO try to see the real him or her, not the person you'd like them to be.
- DO be on your best behavior.
- DO remember your manners. Treat a first date like an interview. We're not saying to be stuffy or overly formal, just polite.
- DO be positive. A good attitude lets a date know you're fun to be around.
- DO dress appropriately.
- DO turn your cellular phone off.

Most Common Dating Mistakes

- 35% Judging your date..."don't judge a book by its cover."
- 27% Having too high expectations for the date
- 25% Spilling your "history" and being too honest
- 13% Talking too much

- DO pull the chair out for a lady or open the car door. Chivalry is NOT dead.
- DO be honest, be yourself and don't play games.
- DO listen.

First Date Don'ts

A few basics that will help avoid first date disasters:

- DON'T be late. One of the quickest ways to sabotage a date is to show up late. Tardiness sends out a message that says, "You're not really important so I didn't make much of an effort to be on time." A great mantra for all aspects of life, including dating is...*if you're not exactly on time (or early), you're late.*
- DON'T talk about yourself all the time.
- DON'T refer to your past dates or talk about past relationships. That doesn't belong in the first date.
- DON'T order spaghetti — it's just not pretty.
- DON'T try too hard. If there's a lull in the conversation, just let it be.
- DON'T wear too much makeup, cologne or perfume.
- DON'T get drunk!
- DON'T prejudge. It takes time to really get to know someone.
- DON'T worry or fret about what they are thinking about you.
- DON'T say, "Oh, you're not at all what I was expecting."

How to Tell If They're Interested or Not

It's really quite simple. There will be lots of clues, primarily given through body language. Don't worry, you don't have to get up close and check to see if their pupils are dilated. It's much easier than that. The non-verbal signals are pretty much the same in both men and women. Here's a quick checklist to help you gauge the chemistry clues:

- Are they smiling at you often?
- Do they compliment you?
- Are they making lots of eye contact or looking around the room?
- Are they leaning toward you?
- Do they try to make body contact, perhaps by touching your arm or putting their arm behind your back to walk you forward?
- Do they seem attentive and interested in what you are saying? Are they nodding a lot?
- Do they make reference to doing something together in the future?

Clues That They're Not Interested

- They look around the room a lot and don't make eye contact. (Even worse, they're checking out other people.)
- They talk about how busy they are, hinting that they don't really have time to date you.
- They talk all the time on the cell phone and ignore you — unacceptable even for a doctor.

The End of the Date

So the date is coming to a close and that confident, funny, super-sexy self that cruised through lunch just flew out the window leaving behind the insecure you.

Now what?

You realize there is a smidgen of a chance that you could be rejected at this point. Or perhaps you're the one who is going to say, "no thanks." Either way, this is often the part of the date that most people dislike.

It's important to be straightforward, however you feel about the other person. This might be a great time to thank your date for a wonderful lunch and leave it at that. If this person isn't right for you, then it's better to deal with it now.

So be honest. Tell them whether you're interested in seeing them again or not. Most people appreciate it when you speak your mind, but make sure you don't just dump your feelings on them. Be responsible and kind.

Let Them Down Gracefully

The great thing about having a lunch date is that if you're not having a good time, returning to work gives you a great out without having to invent some lame excuse. If you really don't want to see the other person again, be honest, but not brutally so. Nobody likes to be rejected, so tell them you enjoyed their company but must get back to work.

If you don't ask for another date, the person will assume you're not interested. Whether it's an *It's Just Lunch* date or you're going it alone, *please don't say,* "I'll call you" if you know you won't. There is nothing worse than waiting around for someone to call. It's better to say nothing than to lead someone on. You wouldn't want someone to do that to you, now would you?

Asking for Another Date

If you've had a good time and you really like them, what do you need to do to seal the deal? How exactly do you leave it? Do you linger in the parking lot, lips puckered, waiting for your date to plant one? Or do you sit in the car talking incessantly for an hour or more, too afraid to make the first move?

Hopefully, you'll do neither. If you had a good time, don't be afraid to say so. Be as enthusiastic as you feel. Say, "I had a great time and I'd love to do it again soon." Then hand them one of your business cards. That way the ball is in their court and they'll call if interested. If you exchange cards, you can rest assured that you both like each other enough to go on another date.

Most women usually expect to hear from a man the next day. And based on our surveys, virtually all men will call within 48 hours if they are interested in seeing their date again. We recommend calling the day after to say thank you or to indicate you'd like to go on another date.

To Kiss or Not to Kiss?

There's really no hard rule when it comes to kissing. We know some women who find it inappropriate to kiss on a first date, and then again we know others who think it's perfectly natural, depending on how the date went. If it's a lunch date, it's probably best to just give each other a hug goodbye. If you've been out for drinks or dinner, let your intuition guide you.

Before you even go in for anything physical, you must first establish that the person you desire wants to be touched. It's easy to tell; just watch their body language. If in doubt, stay away until you receive stronger signals. Just leave it at a hug or a peck on the cheek. Strong sexual advances too early can be a turnoff, even for guys. So trust your instincts.

Five Things to Say If You Want to See Them Again

1. "I had a great time. Would you like to get together again soon?"
2. "Would you be interested in dinner next time?"
3. "This was a great lunch! I'd like to get to know you better."
4. "I'm going hiking on Saturday and would love for you to join me."
5. "Now that the hard part is out of the way, are you interested in going out again?"

Five Things to Say When You're Not Interested

1. "The best of luck and fun in your future dates. Thanks again."
2. "I can see us becoming friends. I'd like to invite you to my next party."
3. "I had a good time, but I just don't think we have that much in common." (Very politely point out the differences between your lifestyles, interests, etc., which will show why you're not a good match.)
4. "I have a friend you might like, can I give him/her your number?"
5. "I feel that the chemistry just isn't quite right between us." (This implies it's a mutual thing.)

A Second Chance?

Well, how did it go? At this point you could be in one of three places. Either you're excited and really want to see them again, or you're convinced that this is not the right person for you. Or perhaps you're unsure about how you feel.

Before you press your built-in reject button, remember that you only need to determine whether or not you want to see them for a second date. So, stop right there!

While first impressions are important — and your time is precious — there is a point to giving someone a second chance. A lot of people suffer from first-date jitters. In fact, fear is the number one cause for first-date disasters and often leads to over-talking or out-of-character shyness.

We usually recommend two or three dates before you rule someone out completely, unless they happened to show up with facial tattoos and a pet snake. By the third date, you'll have gathered enough information to make a solid assessment.

At that point there are two areas you should look at.

The first is compatibility. Do you have things in common? Then, it's a good idea to check in with your own instincts. Ask yourself, "How do they make me feel inside? Are they genuine and trustworthy? Do they treat me with kindness and consideration?"

Trust your instincts, and you'll be surprised at how perceptive you really are.

An instinctive "gut" feeling can draw you to Mr. or Ms. Right even if they don't match all your criteria on paper. You probably have friends who are with partners who you never thought they'd be with. What brings people like that together? They trusted their "gut."

Basically, we all want the same things in a partner: honesty, trust, good communication, confidence, fun and understanding. If we can add chemistry to that, then bingo!

All that's left to work out is the timing. Is this person ready to commit, and does he or she want to share these qualities with you?

The Lists

The Five Best Places for a Lunch or Brunch First Date

Blue Moon Pizza
2359 Windy Hill Rd. S.E. Ste. 100, Marietta
(770) 984-2444
Enjoy the city's best pizza made with the finest freshest ingredients. They offer charming service in a romantic setting, featuring jazz and blues in the background.

Bajarito's
3877 Peachtree Rd., Atlanta
(404) 239-9727 • www.puravidatapas.com
The cheery staff serves fantastic Mexican-Southwestern burritos and tapas. A great location for a casual date.

Atmosphere
1620 Piedmont Ave., Atlanta
(678) 702-1620 • www.atmospherebistro.com
Set in a beautifully charming cottage, this friendly French restaurant has great food and a relaxed, inviting elegance.

Miro's Garden
1150B Euclid Ave., Atlanta
(404) 221-1604

Set in a sweet little indoor courtyard, complete with a fountain and an interior reminiscent of the Cubist painter Joan Miro, this a great place for a first encounter.

Einstein's
1077 Juniper St., Atlanta
(404) 876-7925

Enjoy Sunday brunch at this fun local favorite in the heart of midtown. In the summertime, be sure to dine on the patio.

Five Best Places for After-Work Drinks and Conversation

Front Page News (Little Five Point)
353 Moreland Ave., N.E., Atlanta
(404) 475-7777
Other locations: 1104 Crescent Ave. • www.fpnnews.com

Visit the French Quarter without driving to New Orleans! Sit on the patio next to the fountain and order the Cajun egg rolls (a house favorite) and a signature martini.

McCormick & Schmick's
CNN Center, 190 Marietta St. N.W., Atlanta
(404) 521-1236 • www.mccormickandschmicks.com

Overlooking Centennial Park, this after-work spot draws upscale professionals who know how to loosen their ties when the workday is over.

Park Tavern
500 10th St. N.E., Atlanta
(404) 249-0001 • www.parktavern.com

With an expansive patio overlooking Piedmont Park, this tavern attracts singles year-round. The small brick fireplaces make it a romantic spot. Try the buffalo burger!

City Grill
59 Hurt Plz. S.E., Atlanta
(404) 524-2489 • www.citygrillatlanta.com

Located on several levels of a former Federal Reserve Bank, *City Grill* attracts hordes of after-work martini drinkers and diners who appreciate a taste of old-world style.

Toulouse
2293 Peachtree Rd. N.E., Atlanta
(404) 351-9533 • www.toulouserestaurant.com

Featuring a quaint patio and one of the most impressive wine lists in Atlanta, this conveniently located restaurant is a popular after-work spot. Casual yet divine!

Five Best Places for a First Dinner Date

Pricci
500 Pharr Rd., Atlanta
(404) 237-2941
www.buckheadrestaurants.com/pricci/index.html

First impressions are lasting ones, so make sure that you make a great one by taking your date to a restaurant serving some of the finest Italian food that Atlanta has to offer.

Violette
2948 Clairmont Rd. N.E., Atlanta
(404) 633-3363 • www.violetterestaurant.com

Offering the kind of romantic charm that's sometimes hard to find these days, *Violette* is a great place to sit and enjoy French cooking at its romantic best.

Vinings Inn
3011 Paces Mill Rd. N.W., Atlanta
(770) 438-2282

Vinings Inn features great Southern cooking in a sweet, old home setting. Serving generous portions made just the way your grandma did—with love.

Pleasant Peasant
555 Peachtree St. N.E., Atlanta
(404) 874-3223

Relax in a casual setting reminiscent of old New Orleans and enjoy the great new American cuisine, like pecan-crusted swordfish. Save room for the apple walnut pie!

City Grill
50 Hurt Plaza S.E., Atlanta
(404) 524-2489 • www.citygrillatlanta.com

Dine on Atlanta's best nouveau Southern dishes in an awe-inspiring setting—a former bank lobby. This is a great place to dine, and to see and be seen among the city's elite.

Chapter 7

Beyond the First Date

Well, you both enjoyed your first date experience so much that you've agreed to see each other again. Cool beans! While you might feel somewhat relieved that your dating prospects are finally looking brighter and the hope of finding someone you really like is imminent, just like the first time around, you're probably having similar anxieties about your second date. This time it could be worse because the stakes have been raised — you like this person and the fear of whether or not it will work out has caused that internal voice of doom to rear its ugly head again.

Try to stay in the NOW, the present moment. Don't let your mind get ahead of the actual events here. A second date is a second date is a second date. It's not happy coupledom, it's not the date on which you are guaranteed sex, and it's not the time to determine if he or she is "the one" — it's just an opportunity to spend a little more time with someone you like.

Trust us, you'll know exactly the right moment when the above should take place (if at all), but to relieve your anxiety, you can rest assured it's not on the second date. Remember to stay grounded, keep your expectations in check and your antenna high.

The Second Date

This could be the "make or break date" for you, depending upon how smoothly the evening flows. We usually recommend going on at least three dates before you decide not to see someone again. Sometimes it can take two or three meetings before the chemistry kicks in. On the other hand, if you have to give yourself a pep talk every time you go out to meet this person, you might want to consider calling it a day. Going with the flow too long isn't smart. One of you could get emotionally attached and that makes it harder to break it off later. Again, trust your instincts.

As you did before, choose a place where you feel comfortable and one that suits both of your tastes, otherwise you might be distracted and not able to focus your attention on your date.

Hopefully on this date you are both more relaxed and able to open up and reveal some juicy insight into the things that make you the unique and wonderful person that you are. Remember, your aim is to discover as much relevant information about him or her as possible. Take it easy and don't rush things. Remind yourself that perfect people do not exist in this world and everybody has strong and weak traits — you included.

Your goal is to gather some fundamental facts, discover more of his or her personality and notice your chemistry... oh, and have fun! To do that you should:

- Ask questions and listen carefully.
- Let them see the real you. Drop the façade, open up, disclose more detail and be vulnerable.
- Share yourself — express opinions, desires and interests.
- Know what you want — it's the only way you can determine if you are a match. If you are sure that you are not ready to be a step parent, find out if they have children from a previous marriage.
- Try to see them as they truly are, not as the people you want them to be. It's easy to get carried away with the excitement of meeting someone you really like and to place him or her on a pedestal, while losing sight of the real human being underneath it all.

Don't worry if all your questions aren't answered on this date. Give it time and let the information come out naturally. If you need a little help, check out the conversation starters in chapter six. You don't want to appear as if you're conducting a formal interview. At this stage you shouldn't be trying to determine if you've got a life match, so give yourself some room for romance.

What to Do on Date Number Two

You might feel like you have to do something lovely and amazing that will totally blow your date's mind, but it's really not necessary. At this stage you want to spend time alone, one-on-one, to see how you relate to one another and to notice if there's chemistry. You can move on to an adventurous activity or involve other people on your next and subsequent dates. That will give you a chance to see how your main squeeze-to-be gets along with others (an important clue to their personality). But for now, keep it intimate.

Having dinner together is a great idea, especially if you didn't do it on your first rendezvous.

Check out the list at the end of this chapter for a variety of second date ideas. Any of the previous restaurants would be fine too. Whether you're looking for a laugh or good cheap eats; we've got you covered!

Say Goodnight, Gracie

At the end of the date, don't make false promises about what comes next if you know you're not interested in taking the relationship further. Be honest, tell them what you enjoyed about them and let them know you don't feel the chemistry.

Ladies need to know that if a guy doesn't ask to see you again it probably means that he's not interested. In this case, you probably won't hear from him again. *Guys need to know* that women are harder to read and often won't come right out and say if they're not interested. They don't want to hurt a man's feelings and are more likely to make excuses about not being available for another date. The best way to gauge a woman's feelings is to notice her body language (see chapter four). If she makes lots of eye contact, touches your arm and flips her hair then she's definitely keen. If she avoids you like the plague, you've got no chance, my friend.

If it ends, though, don't sweat it. Breathe a sigh of relief that you got out emotionally unscathed, and turn your attention to the 110 million other single men and women out there.

What to Do on Dates Number Three, Four, Five...

If you've made it this far, it probably means that the two of you are "in like," you enjoy being together and are eager to get to know each other better. Time to up the ante and try out a variety of fun activities that put you into all kinds of social situations. In short, you get to play at being partners by experiencing many different things together and seeing how well you fit and work as a team.

Spice up your dating game with some adventurous dates, play games and share activities, or try something simple and romantic like a moonlit walk. After a while, you might want to add in a few mundane activities to keep it real. Let's face it — long-term relationships include daily chores like shopping, taking the dog to the vet or fixing up the yard. Ask your date to hang out with you while you're at it or to help you out with these chores too.

If your long-term goal is to find a fulfilling relationship, you should pay attention at this stage and see how well you make decisions together or handle real-life situations such as dealing with crises or family obligations. Don't over-analyze every result, since that will kill the fun. Just be aware, observe and communicate your feelings. As each date progresses, you'll get a stronger sense of whether or not you are compatible.

Dating Dilemmas

When They Don't Call

If you've had what you thought was an incredible date and they don't call, it's normal to wonder what the heck went wrong. You start to think you imagined the chemistry, and that perhaps there's something wrong with you after all, or maybe blame is your thing and it must have been something you said or did. You're starting to obsess. Stop it! Don't go down that road. It's never pretty.

Who knows what happened? There are lots of reasons — he lost his job and slipped into depression, she's not over her last relationship, he's a non-committer (better you find out now), her self-esteem was too low, he fell down a well — hey, it's possible!

Whatever the reason, it may not have anything to do with you at all. So don't sweat it. Drop your date one follow-up email and if you don't receive a response, cut your emotional ties right away. Remember, there are six billion people on the planet, so even if there was no chemistry connection on his or her part, who cares? Give yourself a pat on the back for taking a chance. There are plenty more fish in the sea, so don't take it personally.

The Perfect Match

While there is no such thing as the perfect person, there *is* an ideal match out there for you, and actually, there are several. To find that special someone, you must first let go of your ideas about finding the perfect person.

Our fantasies are usually about Mr. or Ms. Perfect and often we eliminate Mr. or Ms. Right because they may not reveal all the perfect qualities. The older we get, the more we rationalize our way around things, and it can ultimately mean we never make any decisions. We get hung up on the "what ifs" and feel sure we know how it's going to turn out. The truth is you never know how something is going to turn out. At a certain point, if you determine that you really want to be in a lasting relationship, you will have to take a chance and work through the ups and downs.

Don't lose sight of the valuable lessons you learn while you're dating — you gain self-confidence, a stronger sense of self, a clear idea of what you can and can't compromise. More importantly, as an experienced dater, it becomes much easier for you to identify your soul mate when he or she finally shows up.

So keep the faith. Make sure your goals are clear from the get go, keep an open dialogue, have a no-bull policy, and you might find yourself in love before you know it.

Are We Exclusive?

Some people don't like to bring this subject up for fear of scaring off their new partner, but *until you actually have an agreement to stop seeing other people and focus solely on each other, you shouldn't assume that you are in an exclusive relationship.* The whole point of dating is to try out different people, and neither of you has to limit yourself to one person.

Don't rush into exclusivity until you know for sure that you want to focus solely on this person. If you were interviewing candidates for a partnership at your company, you wouldn't pick the first person who came along, would you? Well, you are the CEO of *your* life and the more potential partners you meet, the easier it will be for you to find your ideal candidate.

While you're interviewing, never stop learning about the opposite sex. Get interested in them. Imagine you're Barbara Walters or Larry King — and study and "interview" your subjects. The more you know about men or women, the better partner you will become. Talk to them, listen to them and most of all laugh with them.

When you decide to be exclusive with someone you've been dating, it's only fair and respectful to let your other dates know that you're no longer available. Don't just disappear out of their lives without so much as a "see ya." Tell them that someone you've been dating has become a serious relationship. Don't forget to mention how much you enjoyed dating them and what you liked about them. Try to leave them feeling good about the whole experience. You could even remain friends.

The Honeymoon Phase

Many relationships start off peachy keen. We've all been there: Every little mannerism is just adorable, every single statement they utter is worthy of a Nobel Prize, they're so understanding, so wonderful, so beautiful, and miraculously you seem to agree on everything. Welcome to the honeymoon phase.

Oh, it's a joyous time in those first three to six months; after all, there's never any bad news. Unfortunately, it can all come to a grinding halt. While you've spent the past several months eating off her plate and hand-feeding her dessert, you suddenly discover that you hate sauteed mushrooms and if you see one more lettuce cup you'll faint. Darn it, you're hungry!

Some relationships survive the end of the honeymoon period, other's fall by the wayside. But there's no need to feel bad if you can't make it past go and your engine loses steam. Believe it or not, that's how love works and this stage of romantic love is nothing more than Mother Nature's way of ensuring reproduction. Anthropologist Helen Fisher, author of *Why We Love*, claims that romantic love has a limited shelf life for a very good reason — we'd all die of sexual exhaustion if it didn't. She believes that romantic love wasn't built to last forever; it's there to fire our engines and get us all to work, making babies and building houses, and to keep us together during the early stages of child rearing. The intense attachment we feel toward each other ensures the survival of the species.

And to think, Hallmark has made a business off this!

So, how do we survive this period and keep the love alive? Well, according to Ms. Fisher, the answer is to do novel things together. Novelty, she says, drives up levels of dopamine — a brain chemical that is associated with arousal, motivation and goal-oriented behavior — the stuff love is made of.

So, there you have it: the answer to everlasting love.

Might we add one more piece of advice, just in case it turns out to be a false start? Pace yourself during this honeymoon stage. Don't drop your whole life because you're in lust. Don't spend every spare moment with your sweetheart and neglect your friends, family, career or self. Friends

---

aren't there to fill in the gaps until that special someone comes along.

Remember, you're in the "getting to know you" stage. You might decide that this is not the right person for you and will have to return to your life. If you've blown off your friends and your work has suffered, don't expect to find things exactly the way you left them. Also, keeping your own life going while you are in the honeymoon phase takes the pressure off the other person "to be your everything."

You Can't Hurry Love: Is This Going Anywhere?

So, you've been out with your new sweetheart several times, but you're still unsure if the relationship is going anywhere and you find yourself wondering if this person could be "the one." How do you know she is right for you? Will he tell you he cares, will he show you he cares or will he only tell others he wants you in his life?

Timing is everything in a relationship. Some people take time to let things develop before making any serious commitments, while others jump right in and grab the bull by the horns. If you're not going at the same pace, there could be a clash. The truth of the matter is you're ready when you're ready and not a moment before. Try to let the relationship evolve at a natural pace without bulldozing ahead just because you're "primed" or imposing too many expectations on whether or not this can last forever.

Sometimes it can start off hot and heavy, but later you find out you're totally wrong for each other. Or you can start dating someone who may not be your usual type, but over time you fall for him anyway. Give it time to develop and you could be surprised.

You Have Passed Go: Sail Away with Your Sweetheart

Along the way there will be lots of positive signs if things are progressing nicely. These little gems have been culled from thousands of ex-clients who now are happily married:

- You can't stop thinking about each other when you're apart.
- He asks you what you would like, then does it.
- She can make you laugh and lift your spirits.
- He is caring and considerate, asks for and listens to your opinions and feelings.
- You communicate easily and can talk about a variety of things.

- You work together to solve problems.
- You accept each other's differences and can agree to disagree without resentment.
- She is an independent thinker and has her own thoughts and opinions, not just agreeing with yours.
- He is open and comfortable talking about himself.
- She is a well-adjusted, balanced person with a full, interesting life.
- You respect, admire and appreciate each other.

Warning Signs: Promptly Hit the Reject Button
- One of you makes all the effort to make plans.
- Her attention is inconsistent.
- She breaks dates often or cancels at the last minute.
- He doesn't call when he says he will, is frequently late or doesn't show up at all.
- He answers every cell phone call, regardless of where you are.
- He prefers spending time on the golf course with his buddies over taking you out.
- His eyes are wandering around the room checking out other women.
- She drinks more than three alcoholic beverages in an evening.
- He has controlling behavior, is angry or jealous and wants everything to go his way.
- She is neurotic about money and counts every penny, or is a compulsive spender and blows large sums of money frequently.
- He is dishonest or is reluctant to open up about past relationships.
- She is a loner and has no one in her life but you.

Wow, we've covered a lot in this chapter. Great ideas that will keep your dating journey fun and interesting, some of the dilemmas you might face along the way, the stages of hooking up and the signs to watch for on the road to a successful relationship.

You're fully armed with everything you need to do some honest evaluating of the whole experience and decide if you want to continue building this new relationship. The next step? Going steady.

The Lists

Five Best Places for a Second Dinner Date

Nickiemoto's Midtown
990 Piedmont Ave., Atlanta
(404) 253-2010

Sushi with an attitude! Located in trendy midtown, this sushi bar is a departure from the standard earth-toned, bamboo-screened venue. Check out the Monday night drag show!

Prime
3393 Peachtree Rd., N.E., Atlanta
(404) 812-0555 • www.heretoserverestaurants.com

After browsing the upscale shops in Lenox Square Mall, drop by for a gourmet meal and top-notch service. *Prime* is known for beef, but it also serves sushi and seafood.

Twist
Phipps Plaza, 3500 Peachtree Rd., Atlanta
(404) 869-1191 • www.heretoserverestaurants.com

Surrounded by Atlanta's finest boutiques, this chic restaurant is popular with the beautiful people and features mouthwatering tapas and acclaimed sushi. Dress to impress!

Benihana
229 Peachtree St., N.E., Atlanta
(404) 522-9629 • www.benihana.com

With all the knife throwing and cooking in the open kitchens, it's hard for you and your date not to be entertained at this old favorite.

Spice
793 Juniper St., Atlanta
(404) 875-4242 • www.spicerestaurant.com

This chic midtown hot spot is the place where the ultra-hip gather for wine tasting and fabulous cuisine. The modern décor is accented by an impressive art collection.

Five Best Cheap Dates

The Flying Biscuit Café
1655 McLendon Ave., Atlanta
Other locations: Piedmont Ave.
(404) 687-8888 • www.flyingbiscuit.com

A twist on the classic southern breakfast, this favorite serves everything from fried green tomatoes to orange-scented French toast. But come early, they don't take reservations!

Taqueria del Sol
1200 Howell Mill Rd. N.W., Atlanta
(404) 352-5811 • www.taqueriadelsol.com

This renovated meat packing plant draws crowds from all over. Don't let the cafeteria-style seating and low prices fool youæit's one of Atlanta's best Mexican restaurants.

Fellini's Pizza
2809 Peachtree Rd., N.E., Atlanta
(404) 266-0082

Who says you can't get great pizza south of New York? This cafeteria-style pizzeria in Buckhead makes the best hand-tossed pizza everæand it won't break the bank.

Front Page News (Little Five Point)
353 Moreland Ave., Atlanta
Other locations: 1104 Crescent Ave. N.E.
(404) 475-7777 • www.fpnnews.com

Visit New Orleans without paying for the flight into the Crescent City. Don't miss the Cajun egg rolls! And make sure that you get a seat on the patio next to the fountain.

Eats
600 Ponce De Leon Ave. N.E., Atlanta
(404) 888-9149

Jerk chicken and collard greens are done right at this cafeteria-style eatery. Old, young, trendy, and traditional come here strictly for the food. (Try creating your own pasta!)

Five Best Creative Dates

Picnic in Piedmont Park
400 Park Dr., N.E., Atlanta • www.piedmontpark.org

There's plenty of open space under the majestic trees. Lay down a blanket, people watch, and snuggle up close.

Wired & Fired
994 Virginia Ave. N.E., Atlanta
(404) 885-1024 • www.wiredfired.com

This "pottery playhouse" has been heating up Atlanta since 1996. Get your hands dirty and create something memorable with your date.

Chattahoochee River Walk
See website for trails and park map • www.nps.gov

Take your date to a beautiful display of nature. Raft through the rocky shoals, enjoy a Sunday afternoon picnic, or walk hand-in-hand along one of the many trails.

Echo Lounge
551 Flat Shoals Ave. S.E., Atlanta
(404) 681-3600

Buy tickets for an upcoming show. Who knows? You might discover a cutting-edge band before it hits the big time and starts playing in stadiums!

Atlanta Botanical Gardens
1345 Piedmont Ave. N.E., Atlanta
(404) 876-5859 • www.atlantabotanicalgarden.org

Let romance bloom in the midst of the planet's most exquisite flowers. With seasonal exhibits, this museum is a must-see year round—unless you suffer from hay fever!

Five Best Places for Coffee and Dessert

San Francisco Coffee Roasting Company
664 N. Highland Ave. N.E., Atlanta
Call for other locations.
(404) 607-8082

Looking for a great neighborhood coffeehouse? This java joint has everything you'll need—even die-hard *Starbuck's* fans won't be disappointed.

Cool Beans Coffee Roasters
31 Mill St., Marietta Square, Marietta
(770) 422-9866 • www.coolbeanscoffeeroasters.com

This shop roasts its own coffee beans. The coffee is super-fresh, and the atmosphere is mellow—even a little bit beatnik. Sit and chat or enjoy a game of chess.

Café Intermezzo
4505 Ashford Dunwoody Rd. N.E., Atlanta
Other locations: Peachtree Rd. N.E.
(770) 396-1344

For the perfect end to an intimate evening, drop by for after-dinner conversation and dessert. Don't miss the cheesecake!

Dailey's
7 International Blvd. N.E., Atlanta
(404) 681-3303 • www.daileysrestaurant.com

This 1950's-style lounge is a great place to snuggle up with your date on one of the comfy leather couches, sip a cappuccino, and enjoy the live jazz.

Corner Bakery Café
3368 Peachtree Rd. N.E., Atlanta
Call for other locations.
(404) 816-5100 • www.cornerbakery.com

Its friendly staff and Frank Sinatra tunes really do remind you of an old Italian corner bakery. Try a perky espresso and a scrumptious dessert.

Five Best Places for a Laugh

The Punchline
280 Hilderbrand Dr., Atlanta
(404) 252-LAFF • www.punchline.com

An old standby providing Atlanta with the best stand-up comedy acts for the past 22 years. Reservations are highly recommended, and absolutely required for weekend shows.

Whole World Theatre Co.
1214-16 Spring St. N.W., Atlanta
(404) 817-7529 • www.wholeworldtheatre.com

Can't get a ticket to see show? No worries. You can watch live improv on the big screen TV — and it's free. A laugh and a cheap night out — what more could you ask for?

Dad's Garage Theatre Company
280 Elizabeth St. N.E., Atlanta
(404) 523-2144 • www.dadsgarage.com

Dad's Garage is a non-profit, low-key venue where you drink and watch award-winning comedy improv and never-before-seen plays. The Theatre even has a kids' show.

Laughing Matters
173 Cleveland Ave. S.E., Atlanta
(404) 225-5000 • www.laughingmatters.com

Laughing Matters is the innovative place, offering award-winning improv shows, private murder mystery events and classes in communication skills.

Improv in the Park
Lake lawn area, Piedmont Park
400 Park Dr. N.E., Atlanta • www.piedmontpark.org

Free comedy shows are served up on Thursday evenings from late April through May. Large crowds come for hearty belly laughs from some of Atlanta's best comedians.

Ten Great Dates

Your next date is rapidly approaching and you still haven't figured out what you're going to do. The last thing you want is to find yourself in the car or on the phone in a never-ending volley of, "Uh, I don't know, what do you want to do?"

We feel your pain, honestly. To help ease it, we've come up with a countdown of the top 10 date ideas that'll make you look really good. We've covered everything you'll need to complete the mission, so no excuses.

#10. Saturday Night at the Drive-In
The Varsity
61 North Ave. N.W., Atlanta
(404) 881-1706

Get your car detailed, pick up your date, and enjoy a blast from the past with curbside service at the world's largest drive-in. Wash those grilled chili dogs and onion rings down with a frosted orange and make sure that you bring along some peppermint breath mints to share. (And don't forget the popcorn!)

#9. Helicopter Tour of Atlanta
Humes McCoy Aviation
570 Piedmont Ave., N.E., Hanger 54156, Atlanta
(877) 723-5898 • www.humesmccoyaviation.net

Tour the city with Atlanta's biggest and most reputable aviation company. You can create your own flight path—so why not begin near your neighborhood and end up at your favorite restaurant?

#8. Stone Mountain Park
Hwy. 78 E, Exit 8, Stone Mountain.
(770) 498-5690

Spend a day together in the country at Stone Mountain Park. Take a hike, explore the 1870's old town, ride the train, and take the sky lift to see the memorial stone carving of three Confederate heroes. And when you're tired and hungry, stop at *Miss Katie's Sideboard Restaurant* and enjoy a home-style Southern dinner.

#7. Chateau Elan Inn and Winery
6060 Golf Club Dr., Braselton
(800) 233-WINE

Spend a day at the world-class resort and winery *Chateau Elan*. Start off with a complimentary tour and wine tasting. Then treat yourself and your date to a relaxing European-style facial. Top that off with dinner at one of the six restaurants featured at this upscale resort and vineyard.

#6. Take a Ride on the Wild Side
Six Flags Over Georgia
7561 Riverside Pkwy @ Interstate 20, Austell
(770) 948-9290

When's the last time you screamed your head off just for fun? Grab some cotton candy, your date's hand, and take a wild ride. Get wet together on the *Log Flume* and make yourselves dizzy on the *Georgia Scorcher*. When you need a breather, enjoy a show at one of the open-air stages. Relax and be kids again!

#5. A Day at the Beach
Lake Lanier Islands
6950 Holiday Rd., Buford
(770) 932-7255

On a hot day, rent a sailboat and feel the breeze. Or rent jet skis and race. Or maybe saddle up for a trail ride and explore the island together on scenic trails. Or you can get your hearts pumping at the water park, water slides and wave pool. The options are limitless.

#4. Take Me Out to the Ball Game
Turner Field
755 Hank Aaron Dr. SE., Atlanta
(404) 577-9100

Join 41,000 of your best friends for a hot dog and a beer or two, and cheer Atlanta's home team on to their next pennant. Buy matching hats and shirts and — who knows? — maybe you'll look up and see yourselves on the Big Screen!

#3. Light the Olympic Torch
Centennial Olympic Park
Techwood Dr. and International Blvd., Atlanta
(404) 223-4412

You don't have to be an athlete to enjoy the splendor at the site of the 1996 Summer Olympics. One way to relive the magic is a picnic lunch for two at one of the many free concerts held throughout the year. And be sure to stay for the sunset—it's breathtaking.

#2. Let Life Imitate Art
High Museum of Art
1280 Peachtree St., Atlanta, GA
(404) 733-4550 • www.high.org

Take your date out on Friday night to check out the exhibitions and collections at Atlanta's home to the works of the great European and American masters. Participate in an art-making workshop. Then talk about what you saw (or what you made) over dessert and drinks while you listen to live jazz in the *Robinson Atrium*.

#1. Feed Your Body and Soul
Renew Day Spa & Wellness Center
4347 Shallowford Rd., Marietta
(770) 998-8592

Spend a day being pampered together. Sip a bit of bubbly. Listen to the sounds of a waterfall as a massage gently turns you (and your date) into jello. Get your nails done together and have twin mud facials. Then soak in a hot tub to melt away any traces of tension you might have left.

Chapter 8
Going Steady

You've made it past the three-month stage and you're still happily dating someone. Congratulations! You're moving out of the dating game and into relationship territory.

You no longer have to worry about attracting the opposite sex, going out to bars, getting set up by well-meaning friends, or any of those single life things. What a relief! But, being in a relationship does come with its own set of responsibilities and dilemmas. Working through them together will set the foundation on which to build something wonderful.

In this chapter we'll take a look at some of the fundamental issues and questions you might come across at this stage of the mating game. Things like coping with holidays and birthdays, saying "I love you" and ultimately, determining if he or she is "the one" or at least on the road to becoming that.

Holidating

Ah, 'tis the season of love, generosity, joy to the world and peace on earth... unless of course you're in the early throes of dating. Then it can just as easily feel like you are walking through a mine field of difficult choices with the pressure of family dinners, gift giving and all those parties to attend. You can be pushed right into happy coupledom way too soon or be accused of neglecting your new potential amour in favor of your friends and family.

Add to that the hassle of holiday shopping and the pressure to find the perfect gift — one that won't be deemed inadequate, or worse, be deemed as too much (which might make you come off as needy or desperate). It's no wonder the thought of hibernating suddenly seems very appealing.

So what is the right holiday protocol? After three months of dating, should you invite someone home to Wisconsin where your mother will inevitably express her desire for grandchildren while pulling on the wishbone?

Or will your date get the wrong idea and assume things are getting serious because you're introducing him or her to your folks? (Of course, if they're not invited, they might get offended and think you don't care. Oh, no! What are you going to do?)

In our experience, the top three issues that cause the biggest problems between couples during the holidays are gift giving, family dinners and party etiquette.

To keep you on track, we've put our heads together here at *It's Just Lunch* and come up with a few tips and ideas to help you navigate your way, peacefully, through the dating dilemmas of the holiday season. Our advice, of course, depends on how long you've been dating.

Thanksgiving/Christmas/Chanukah

Less Than Three Months
Spend it with your family and call him or her from home. It's too early to expect that you will spend these family-oriented holidays together. If you're in the same town, you can always invite your date over for dessert later.

Three to Six Months
If you've been dating for more than three months, bringing your partner to a friend's house for dinner is appropriate, but it's still a little early to bring them home to the folks if your parents live out of state. However, if you all live in the same city or reasonably close, it is probably okay. Feel it out.

Six Months Plus
If your new honey hasn't already met your family, now is the time. It can be a little nerve wracking and you might not have much of an appetite for your mom's turkey dinner, so be prepared. If you get invited to a family event, be on your best behavior and dress on the conservative side. Come bearing gifts and offer to do the dishes. Also, pay attention to how your significant other is around his or her family — you'll get a sneak peak of the real person coming out, so take notes!

New Year's Eve

Less than three months
New Year's Eve has taken over from Valentine's Day as the world's most high-pressured and overpriced date night. If you've been together *less than a month*, don't expect anything — continue with your previous plans. If you're doing something where you can bring a date, mention it lightly, but don't be offended if they already have other plans.

If the two of you have been dating for *more than a*

month, feel it out discreetly and make sure you have back-up plans so you don't sit home alone sulking.

Three to Six Months
It's a date. Plan something fun and expect to bring in the New Year with a midnight kiss from your dream date.

Six Months Plus
This is your first New Year together and you're in the sweetest part of the Honeymoon period, so make it special and celebrate your coupledom.

Valentine's Day

Less than three months
Don't even bring it up if you've been dating for a month or less. *If you've been dating for more than a month*, bring it up casually, but don't expect anything.

Three to Six Months
If you've been together this long, it's reasonable to expect to exchange gifts and to enjoy a good dinner together. If one of you isn't up for that, it's likely you're in different places in your relationship.

Six Months Plus
This is a time for somewhat bigger romantic gestures — a special dinner together at a fancier restaurant than you usually go to and an exchange of gifts that are nicer.

Birthdays

Less Than Three Months
Under a month, just wish them a happy birthday and buy them a drink the next time you go out. *If you've been dating more than a month*, bring them a thoughtful (though not necessarily expensive) gift.

Three to Six Months
A nicer gift and/or flowers is reasonable, along with a nice dinner alone or with friends.

Six months plus
Invite a few of your honey's favorite friends and throw a surprise dinner party.

The Gift-Giving Guide

The hassle of fighting your way through all those pushy holiday shoppers is enough to give you a cardiac arrest without the added pressure of getting him or her that perfect gift that says it all.

The key is to plan ahead. It'll save you from rushing out in the last minute, spending extra money and compromising more than you planned.

The best way to figure out an appropriate and well-received gift is to be mindful of your mate's interests, dreams and desires. This will give you all the information you need to find that perfect gift.

It really is the thought that counts, and if you just put a little of it into your gift, it will make a colossal difference.

A husband we know always sends his wife flowers. What makes it so unique is that he hand selects the vase at Neiman's or Pottery Barn, matches it with the perfect card and gives everything to the florist to deliver with a beautiful arrangement. It's the hand selection of the vase and the personalized card (instead of the standard card the florist fills out) that makes it extra special. This is such a cool idea if you're a guy who wants to say thanks for a great date. (Girls, remember most guys do *not* want flowers.)

You don't have to wait for a special occasion to give something thoughtful. A woman we know, who met a man through a dating service, was blown away when he showed up for their second date with a small box of her favorite candy — chocolate dipped strawberries. How did he know? He remembered it was on her profile among her favorite things. Needless to say he won major points for being so thoughtful and going that extra mile to say she was special.

At the end of the day a gift will not make or break your relationship. Good communication will go further in creating a love affair than a piece of jewelry or a set of golf clubs.

What's Appropriate and When?

Less Than Three Months

For the guy or gal you've gone out with a dozen or so times, we suggest starting out with something thoughtful, rather than showy. Spending too much money on someone you just met will make you appear over invested and will make you look needy. They'll feel like they have to reciprocate and that could make them uncomfortable. Keep the gift simple and special.

Gifts for Him
- Melt his heart and bake him brownies.
- Buy him your favorite book and share something you love.
- If he's a sports fan, try a team logo sweatshirt or a golf shirt.

Steer clear of: Anything commitment driven like rings, watches, a mini-break in Hawaii... or anything too personal like nose-hair trimmers!

Gifts for Her
- Homemade CD of her favorite tunes.
- Godiva chocolates and/or flowers.
- Champagne flutes and a good bottle of champagne.

Steer clear of: Jewelry, lingerie or other sexy items and expensive gifts. (Oh, and nose-hair trimmers!)

Three to Six Months
At this point you're heading toward exclusivity, but most likely haven't committed to anything final or met the family yet. This is a pivotal point in the relationship and it's best to celebrate holidays and special occasions with a personal gift and a romantic dinner.

Gifts for Him
- Cook him a romantic dinner for two — wine, candles, soft music, a sexy outfit, the whole enchilada. This will show not only that you care, but that you can cook, too!
- The newest toy or gadget from the Sharper Image (www.sharperimage.com) or Hammacher Schlemmer (www.Hammacher.com). It need not be expensive or over the top.
- If you really like the guy but hate the way he dresses, a designer sweater goes a long way.

Stay clear of: Generic gifts like a wallet or pen. You want to let him know he's special.

Gifts for Her
- Romantic dinner for two at a little French bistro or surprise her with dinner at your place — the works (she'll love the gesture).

- Anything cashmere or pashmina.
- Tickets to the opera or ballet and have a courier deliver them to her office along with flowers. That way she can show off to her friends.

Steer clear of: Clothing. We all know that women love clothes, but don't even go there unless you know the following criteria:
- Her exact taste (unlikely)
- What's *in* for the season (pass). Better to stay well away, unless you happen to work for Gucci.
- Her exact size (too small she'll feel fat, too large she'll think you're saying she's fat, and remember it differs between brands).

Six months plus

Hallelujah! You're madly in love at this point. This is the time when you want your significant other to feel like the most special person in your life. Make your gifts personal, intimate and a true expression of your fabulous unity.

Gifts for Him
- Tickets for two to his favorite sporting event.
- Get him TiVo so he can create his own instant replays while watching the big game.
- A watch with a personal inscription from you

Steer clear of: Don't get him anything you think he *should* have, like a DustBuster or a particular tool, unless he's expressed specific interest in it.

Gifts for Her
- Arrange for a massage therapist to be at her home after a long day at work.
- Get her lingerie or other sexy items. (Warning! These should only be given for Valentine's Day or anniversaries, and are not right for holiday gifts or birthdays — otherwise they are considered gifts for *you*, not her!)
- Say it with diamonds and you've pretty much said everything your girlfriend needs to hear. A bracelet or pendant is appropriate.

When to Whisper Those Three Little Words

There comes a time in a relationship when one of you will

utter those three very important little words. It's a significant moment, often accompanied by fears of rejection, feeling silly, being misunderstood or worse still, pressure.

Don't ever feel pressured to say, "I love you" unless you really mean it. It's better to say that you sincerely care about your significant other than falsely claiming to love her. Lying will inevitably come back to bite you in the butt, so don't even go there.

By the same token, don't force your mate to say or feel it in return because you're afraid he or she doesn't. Saying "I love you" and being in integrity with that statement means you have no demands back. Love is a gift that is given freely and without expectation.

Partners often feel the urge to amplify their feelings by projecting their affection onto one another and in the heat of the moment will blurt things out. But if you're not sure of your feelings and your mate tells you they love you, you must respond honestly.

If you love them, tell them. If you're unsure say, "Thank you for being so open, that makes me feel wonderful." Or say, "That makes me very happy. I really care about you too." If you don't feel the same way be delicate when responding, as it could really hurt the other person.

Don't ever dump your feelings onto your partner by responding with, "don't say that," or, "I don't love you yet," or, "I'm not ready to hear that." It takes courage to be vulnerable, so handle with care and compassion.

Show How You Feel

It's possible to go a long time in a relationship without saying, "I love you." Often, actions speak louder than words and there are many other "little things" that indicate a person's level of affection for another.

Women respond to "little sentiments," those tidbits of information that might seem irrelevant to most men but become benchmarks in a woman's relationship — things like remembering the song that was playing on the radio when you first kissed or her favorite color or flower.

Men respond equally to small gestures. Leaving love notes under his pillow or packing a few power bars and a vitamin drink in his briefcase before he heads off for a long day at work can be extremely touching to a man.

You don't have to spend buckets of money to show your partner that he or she is precious to you. In the same respect, "talk is cheap," and you can throw about "I love yous" like plates at a Greek wedding, but in order for the words to really make an impact, they must be backed up with significant action.

It's important to observe all the non-verbal clues in a relationship too. Determining if someone is right for you lies as much in his or her actions and in what they don't do, as it does in what they say.

Telling your girlfriend that you want to spend more quality time with her and then spending weekends at the golf course just doesn't measure up. As time goes by, your endearments will lose their meaning and your trust will begin to deteriorate.

Pay attention to the special things that touch your girl-friend or boyfriend and make an effort to introduce these into your relationship on a regular basis. It takes effort and mindfulness to create a phenomenal affinity with another person. But it's worth it because ultimately you reap the rewards.

His Needs, Her Needs
Yes, by now we all know that men are from Mars and women are from Venus, but what we haven't quite figured out is how in the heck are we supposed to ever get it together? Here are a few guidelines to help you give each other what men and women need most in a relationship.

All the Dating Dos and Don'ts You'll Ever Need For Men
- DO agree to do things with her friends or family.
- DO listen attentively (lots of eye contact) and be interested in discovering her likes and dislikes.
- DO be affectionate and romantic. Send love notes and flowers, hold hands, give hugs and make loving phone calls.
- DO talk to your girlfriend. It's an important emotional need and you'll learn how to become more compatible through conversation.
- DO be honest and open. Build trust by sharing your thoughts, feelings, habits, likes, dislikes and daily activities.
- DON'T expect her to date you exclusively while you play around.
- DON'T expect sex.

All the Dating Dos and Don'ts
You'll Ever Need for Women

- DO let him go out with his friends.
- DO allow him to withdraw or go into his cave, once in a while, without insisting he talk about it.
- DO engage in recreational activities with him — watch football, play sports, go fishing.
- DO make an effort to look attractive and wear outfits that make you feel great.
- DO give him compliments and let him know he's appreciated.
- DON'T push him into commitment or saying he loves you.
- DON'T try to be who you think he wants you to be — be yourself.
- DON'T try to fix or change him.

Are We Ready for Commitment?

Are you and your partner both emotionally ready for a committed relationship at this time? If one of you is and one of you isn't, you are both wasting your time and energy.

Avoiding this conversation (or choosing to overlook the importance of it) is a major mistake. You could mislead someone into believing there is a future with you, or you might spend months or years fooling yourself with an unavailable partner.

In relationships, as in life, timing is everything. We all get to different stages of emotional growth at different times and there is no right or wrong time for commitment. It happens when you're ready. And for some, it may never come.

Relationship experts believe that we attract people who reflect some part of ourselves, so if you find that you frequently attract non-committal partners, you may have some subconscious motivation not to commit yourself.

One of the greatest benefits of joining a service like *It's Just Lunch* is that most people who register with us are looking for a committed relationship. It's an efficient way to weed out many time wasters, fence sitters and serial daters.

Is This "The One?"

Most people have an idea of what constitutes a desirable mate. We usually get fixated on superficial aspects like

Women Only:

Beware of the fix-and-change phenomena. There's a common pitfall that a lot of women fall into when deciding if their new beau is a Mr. Right candidate.

They focus too much on potential and whether or not a man is marriage material. That gets them into trouble because as soon as they find a man with potential they feel like they have to develop him and turn him into that perfect guy. Perhaps there are several really great things about him, but then there are those two or three little things, and if they could just change that then... get the picture? So they spend the next however many months or years trying to fix him and forget about having fun with him.

Ladies, you've got to give up trying to fix and change your guy. You don't do that to your friends. You accept that they have weaknesses and strengths as well as a whole slew of quirky behaviors. And you love them anyway.

Now, we're not being biased here. It's just that men usually don't do that to women, although there are some exceptions to the rule. (If you're one of them then take heed!) But, in our experience, if a man doesn't like something about a woman he'll either break up or accept her the way she is. He won't stick around for years trying to make her a better person.

A woman, on the other hand, will date a man and ask herself, "Is this who I want to spend the rest of my life with?" If the answer is, "yes, he could be," then she'll try to turn him into Mr. Perfect. If he's a bad communicator, she'll try to open him up and get him to share his feelings. If he's afraid of commitment, she'll try to become all he could ever want.

People don't change unless they want to. Unless he comes to you asking for support, don't take it upon yourself to show him a happier way. You might spend years wasting your time and never get what you really want anyway.

appearance, income or lifestyle and don't give enough thought to the quality of that relationship.

It's emotional intimacy, being able to share your truest, deepest, most vulnerable self with your significant other, which makes us feel loved. Skip judgments based on superficial aspects and focus on how you connect emotionally; how comfortable you are being yourself when you're around them, and how often you laugh and have fun together.

Really, that's all there is to it. If you can read the paragraph above and know in your heart that your partner meets all of these needs and makes you feel great about yourself, then he or she has all the qualities to become your ideal partner. The rest is up to the two of you.

A relationship is like any long-term investment: it requires a great deal of time, effort and devotion. Couples come and go, but real relationships are those that can survive whatever life throws at them. They go through it together and come out closer than before.

One final thing you should ask yourself before you decide that this is the person you want to spend the rest of your life with: Do you both share the same vision for the future?

Do you want the same things or are you at least committed to helping the other fulfill his or her dreams as well as your own? Do you both see yourselves together for many years to come? Can you imagine investing in a house, raising a family and eventually growing old together?

Recognizing Mr. or Ms. Right

Follow the steps that follow and you won't lose your head as you get to know your significant other better. Remain clear and confident and you'll make the right choices.

Before you choose to commit to someone, make sure you have no desperate need for attachment and that you are in a good place with your self-esteem. Be ready to walk away if things don't turn out as planned. Don't try to force a relationship to work or invest time trying to change someone. The whole purpose is to avoid ending up in divorce court. Why would you want to close a deal that has the wrong foundation or missing parts?

If you have seven or eight of the signs below in your relationship, then this could be it! Yeeeehaw!

Nine Signs for Recognizing Mr. or Ms. Right
- You listen to each other.
- You have a strong chemistry connection.
- He or she is a cheerleader for your hopes and dreams.

- You tell them what you want in a relationship and he or she steps up to the plate.
- Your partner is genuine, trustworthy and understanding.
- You can both compromise and work together to resolve disputes.
- You have a similar approach to life (values, morals, goals).
- Your partner shows you kindness, consideration and respect.
- You are focused on each other, not looking around for something better.

A relationship is a two-way street. Don't forget that you need to be all of these things back.

A Final Word

We hope this book has inspired you in some way to get out there and embark upon your dating adventure. We also hope it has helped you to replace any negativity you might have toward dating with faith and enthusiasm. At the risk of sounding like a Hallmark card, anything is possible if you believe. Take a few physical and emotional steps toward making it happen and you'll be amazed how the scales tip in your favor. It's all about attitude — your attitude.

If you're still reluctant to take control of your dating destiny, ask yourself this: If not now, when?

Seriously! This is your life happening, right now. Don't put off love until tomorrow, or it might never come.

Dating is the chance to try a few relationships, see how they fit and decide whether or not you want to make a long-term purchase.

Yes, there are emotions involved. Finding the love of your life means you'll have to take some risks and you could get hurt. But not dating doesn't mean you won't be exposed to emotional pain. Loneliness isn't much fun, either.

Remember, Mr. or Ms. Perfect only exist in the movies. Your goal is to find the perfect union, not the perfect person. The more you date, the more you develop your dating radar. You'll know quickly when a relationship has all the ingredients you're looking for.

Allow yourself to fail as many times as it takes before you prevail. If you find yourself single again, don't worry. There are endless options when it comes to being a proactive dater. Eventually you'll meet "the one." It takes time, so be patient.

You're armed and ready to go out into the world with hundreds of places to go, take or meet potential dates in your city. What more do you need?

Now get out there and have a blast!

The Lists

Five Best Places for Valentine's Day Dates

Ray's on the River Seafood House
6700 Powers Ferry Rd., Atlanta
(770) 955-1187 • www.raysontheriver.com

This romantic Marietta hot spot on the beautiful Chatta-hoochee River has been the setting for many engagement celebrations. (And critics consistently praise the seafood here.)

Vinings Inn
3011 Paces Mill Rd., SE Atlanta
(770) 438-2282 • www.viningsinn.com

A popular watering hole for 30- and 40-somethings, *Vinings Inn* features live music on the weekends. Small rooms and a rocking-chair porch give the bar a cozy atmosphere.

Sun Dial Restaurant & Bar at the Westin Downtown
210 Peachtree St. N.W., Atlanta
(404) 589-7506 • www.sundialrestaurant.com

The Westin may be full of tourists, but the rotating bar on top is a favorite for locals as well. Ride the glass elevator and hold your honey tight as you take in the stunning view.

Canoe
4199 Paces Ferry Rd. N.W., Atlanta
(770) 432-2663 • www.canoe-atl.com

Its beautiful historic riverside setting makes it the perfect spot for romance. This award-winning gem of a restaurant offers tasty American cuisine served with artistry and style.

Nava
3060 Peachtree Rd. N.W., Atlanta
(404) 240-1984 • www.buckheadrestaurants.com/nava/

Nava offers a total Southwestern experience. Its innovative menu features delicious dishes such as suncorn-crusted snapper and cowboy-cut beef tenderloin.

Five Best Special-Occasion Restaurants

Spice
793 Juniper St., Atlanta
(404) 875-4242

Spice up your night at this trendy, sexy, venue specializing in delicious seafood with an Asian influence. Save room for the warm chocolate truffle and roasted banana ice cream.

Capital Grille
255 E. Paces Ferry Rd. N.E., Atlanta
(404) 262-1162 • www.thecapitalgrille.com

This upscale restaurant serves mouth-watering steaks, fresh seafood and heavenly desserts. An ideal choice for that special date.

Ray's on the River Seafood House
6700 Powers Ferry Rd., Atlanta
(770) 955-1187 • www.raysontheriver.com

Visit this Marietta hot spot on the beautiful Chattahoochee River for critically acclaimed seafood served in a romantic setting.

Kyma
3085 Piedmont Rd. N.E., Atlanta
(404) 262-0702 • www.buckheadrestaurants.com/kyma

Kyma offers a lounge-like urban take on classic Mediterranean seafood. From the stark, ultra-modern blue and white décor to the attentive staff, *Kyma* never fails to impress.

Dante's Down the Hatch
3380 Peachtree Rd. N.E., Atlanta
(404) 266-1600 • www.dantesdownthehatch.com

Not your run of the mill fondue joint, this one's got live alligators! The low-lit rooms are designed like an abandoned ship. With live jazz nightly, *Dante's* is an absolute *must*!

Five Best Places to Find Gifts They'll Love

Metropolitan Deluxe
3500 Peachtree Rd. N.E., Atlanta
(404) 812-3414 • www.metropolitandeluxe.com

The eclectic mix of home accents, furniture, beautiful fresh flowers, unique cards, and lots of pampering products, will give you a million great gift ideas in a one-stop shop.

Mitzi & Romano
1038 N. Highland, Atlanta
(404) 876-7228

Offering everything from *au courant* designers to something for the more conservative. You can pick up *Seven* and *Citizen* jeans, or *Michael Stars* and *James Pearse* tees here.

Highland Gifts for Men
1002 Virginia Ave. N.E., Atlanta
(404) 817-0470

If you're dating the man who has everything this store is for you. Choose from unique shaving kits, bar ware, tools and cool gadgets he loves (but would never buy for himself).

Blue Genes
3400 Around Lenox Dr. N.E., Atlanta
(404) 231-3400 • www.bluegenesatlanta.com

Blue Genes recently added a men's store to the already established women's boutique. Choose urban designer clothing that will place you at the forefront of fashion.

The Purple Hall
1037 N Highland Ave. N.E., Atlanta
(404) 815-1077

Their moderately priced glassware, scented candles, hand towels, and other accessories make it a great place to find the perfect house warming, birthday, or anniversary gift.

Appendix

What's Your Dating IQ?

Take our dating quiz and see how your answers compare to those of other singles nationwide.

1. At what point would you introduce someone to your best friends?
   a. After 3 dates
   b. More than 5
   c. After 5 dates
   d. After 1 date

2. Women Only! Have you ever asked a man out on a date?
   a. Yes
   b. No

3. If not, why?
   a. Fear of rejection; I'd be crushed if he said no.
   b. I'm old fashioned — the man should do the asking.
   c. I'm worried I would appear desperate.
   d. I'm too shy; I'd be tongue-tied.
   e. No need, I always get asked.

4. Which date option do you think would most entice a man?
   a. Dinner
   b. A movie
   c. A drink after work
   d. A sporting event
   e. Lunch
   f. A concert

5. If you do the inviting, would you expect to pay for the date?
   a. I'd be prepared to pay, unless he offered.
   b. Of course, I'd pay.
   c. No, the man should pay, no matter what.

6. After how many dates would you utter the six magic words, "Would you like to come in?"
   a. After we're officially a couple.
   b. After a third date.
   c. Never. I'd wait until the man asks to come in.
   d. After the first date.

7. Men Only! Has a woman ever asked you out on a date?
   a. Yes
   b. No

8. How do you feel about a woman asking you out for a date?
   a. I'm flattered; it's a real turn-on.
   b. Depends on the woman.
   c. Too aggressive; not my type.
   d. Regret that I didn't take the lead.

9. What do you think it means when a woman invites you in after a first date?
   a. Yippee, I've scored a home run!
   b. Does she want coffee... or something else?
   c. I'm afraid to say no, it might hurt her feelings.
   d. Makes me nervous.

Both sexes from this point...

10. At what point in a relationship would you feel comfortable bringing your significant other home for the holidays?
    a. Dating at least two months.
    b. Dating for at least a month.
    c. Dating at least six months.
    d. With my family? Never!
    e. After dating for at least two weeks.

11. Of all the following, I would be LEAST interested in dating:
    a. My friend's ex
    b. A co-worker
    c. A client
    d. Someone my mother wants to set me up with

12. After how many dates would you use the term "boyfriend" or "girlfriend?"
    a. 7 - 9 dates
    b. 5 - 6 dates
    c. more than 10 dates
    d. 3 - 4 dates

13. You are meeting your significant other's parents for the first time during the holidays. Which would you do?
    a. Bring a card, candy, flowers, bottle of wine or other similar gift.
    b. Pick out a modest gift for the two of them.
    c. Come empty handed, after all, we're just meeting for the first time.
    d. Do some research and purchase something exceptional.
    e. Sign your name to your boyfriend's/girlfriend's gift.

14. On a first date, I'd prefer:
    a. A casual lunch date
    b. Drinks after work
    c. A dressy dinner or other formal affair
    d. A concert, play or movie

15. You've been dating for a couple of weeks. How many times a day should you be calling your new boyfriend/girlfriend before 6 P.M.?
    a. You'd never think to call during work hours.
    b. Once. You want to check in and see how their day is going.
    c. 2 – 3 times. You just want to let them know you're thinking about them.

d. More than 4 times. You're thinking about
them every minute.

16. The shoes a person is wearing on a date tell the
other:
    a. About their personality.
    b. How in tune that person is with fashion.
    c. About their personal hygiene.
    d. How much money they have.

17. Of all the dating conversation killers, the worst
would have to be:
    a. Marriage
    b. Politics
    c. Past relationships
    d. Dieting/body image

18. What's the biggest turnoff on a first date?
    a. Talking only about oneself.
    b. Bad manners.
    c. Poor eye contact.

19. Which dating mistake do you think is the most
common?
    a. Talking too much.
    b. Having too high expectations for the date.
    c. Judging your date like a "book by its
       cover."
    d. Spilling your "history" and being too
       honest.

20. If you'd like to go on a second date, how do you
pursue him/her?
    a. Wait to be pursued.
    b. Call the next day.
    c. Email them the same night as the date.
    d. Wait 3 – 4 days, then call.

See How You Compare!
Below are our national averages based on various surveys
of singles.
    1. a. 46%, b. 17%, c. 30%, d. 7%
    2. a. 58%, b. 42%
    3. a. 25%, b. 39%, c. 18%, d. 9% e. 9%
    4. a. 12%, b. 3%, c. 44%, d. 32%, e. 7%, f. 2%

5. a. 70%, b. 24%, c. 6%
6. a. 24%, b. 59%, c. 7%, d. 11%
7. a. 67%, b. 33%
8. a. 63%, b. 34%, c. 1%, d. 1%
9. a. 18%, b. 62%, c. 7%, d. 14%
10. a. 37%, b. 19%, c. 34%, d. 3%, e. 7%
11. a. 60%, b. 14%, c. 8%, d. 17%
12. a. 25%, b. 22%, c. 47%, d. 6%
13. a. 60%, b. 18%, c. 9%, d. 12%, e. 1%
14. a. 44%, b. 43%, c. 4%, d. 8%
15. a. 44%, b. 52%, c. 4%, d. 0%
16. a. 45%, b. 39%, c. 12%, d. 4%
17. a. 15%, b. 15%, c. 49%, d. 21%
18. a. 35%, b. 51%, c. 10%
19. a. 13%, b. 27%, c. 35%, d. 25%
20. a. 28%, b. 38%, c. 7%, d. 27%

To participate in one of our dating surveys, which change each month, go to www.itsjustlunch.com.

About
the Author

Michelle Brown is the Director of the It's Just Lunch office in Atlanta. Michelle has appeared on 95.5 THE BEAT and has also been featured on The Today Show. She and her team coordinate thousands of fun dates each year.

Here's how to reach the It's Just Lunch office nearest you

Office	Phone
Headquarters	619.234.7200
Albany	518.482.8400
Albuquerque	505.244.1050
Ann Arbor	734.327.2700
Atlanta	404.588.2700
Atlanta Suburbs	770.590.4910
Austin	512.476.5566
Baltimore	410.659.6699
Birmingham	205.986.6050
Buffalo	716.839.2787
Central PA	570.522.9922
Charlotte	704.332.6081
Chicago	312.644.9999
Chicago Suburbs	630.775.6633
Cincinnati	513.929.4499
Cleveland	216.830.9999
Columbus	614.233.9999
Dallas	972.991.4161
Denver	303.292.2600
Detroit Suburbs	248.273.1000
Ft.Lauderdale/Boca Raton	954.725.8500
Ft.Lee, NJ	201.363.9594
Ft. Myers	239.939.3900
Ft. Worth	817.870.9999
Grand Rapids	616.235.6700
Harrisburg	717.234.3400
Honolulu	808.532.7300
Houston	713.572.0900
Huntsville	256.519.3600
Jacksonville	904.281.0277
Kansas City	816.421.5600
Las Vegas	702.436.4600
LA Century City	310.229.9393
LA South Bay	310.937.8200
LA The Valley	818.548.9988
Miami	305.381.8888
Milwaukee	414.224.9600
Minneapolis	612.376.7373
Naples	239.597.4100
Nashville	615.312.9700

New York City 212.750.8899
No. Virginia 703.506.6767
Omaha 402.991.9388
Orange County 949.251.9494
Orlando 407.835.8888
Palm Beach County 561.799.9955
Philadelphia 215.772.9999
Phoenix 602.279.3366
Phoenix—East Valley 480.785.4949
Pittsburgh 412.263.2499
Portland 503.248.9995
Raleigh-Durham 919.836.9199
Sacramento 916.564.1400
San Antonio 210.525.9988
San Diego Downtown 619.232.8999
San Diego County 760.268.0004
San Francisco 415.989.9500
Sarasota 941.362.7702
Scottsdale 480.730.6023
Silicon Valley 650.969.1100
St. Louis 314.863.7300
St. Paul 651.228.0070
Seattle 206.340.0100
Tampa 813.204.9688
Tucson 520.299.6338
Walnut Creek 925.287.8700
Washington, D.C. 202.466.6699
West Texas 806.687.4440
Wilmington, DE 302.651.9999

International
Singapore 65.6536.0100
Toronto 416.703.3900

Call Today, Date Tomorrow

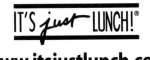

www.itsjustlunch.com

dating for busy professionals®